You Are *Not* Going to Heaven
(and why it doesn't matter)

You Are *Not* Going to Heaven (and why it doesn't matter)

WES BERGEN

WIPF & STOCK · Eugene, Oregon

YOU ARE *NOT* GOING TO HEAVEN (AND WHY IT DOESN'T MATTER)

Copyright © 2013 Wes Bergen. All rights reserved. Except for brief quotations in critical publications or reviews, no part of this book may be reproduced in any manner without prior written permission from the publisher. Write: Permissions, Wipf and Stock Publishers, 199 W. 8th Ave., Suite 3, Eugene, OR 97401.

Wipf & Stock
An Imprint of Wipf and Stock Publishers
199 W. 8th Ave., Suite 3
Eugene, OR 97401
www.wipfandstock.com

ISBN 13: 978-1-62032-612-1

Manufactured in the U.S.A.

All scripture quotations, unless otherwise indicated, are taken from the New Revised Standard Version Bible, copyright 1989, Division of Christian Education of the National Council of the Churches of Christ in the United States of America. Used by permission. All rights reserved.

For Deb, Erin, and John
who make life worthwhile.

Contents

Foreword / ix
Acknowledgments / xi

1. Introduction / 1
2. Old Testament—the bad news / 15
3. New Testament—the bad news / 39
4. Old Testament—the good news / 58
   - a) We're all in this together / 58
   - b) Contentment / 71
   - c) The Genesis model / 81
   - d) Limits and warnings about militarism / 89
   - e) Wisdom / 98
   - f) Recognizing the whole range of human emotions / 107
   - g) God / 113
5. New Testament—the good news / 120
   - a) Development of Old Testament themes / 120
   - b) Additional themes / 141
6. Conclusion / 157

Foreword

IN 1957, IN A remote location in the Arizona desert, a small silver spacecraft landed and buried itself in the earth. This book is not about that event.

Acknowledgments

So much of who I am and what I know has come out of interaction with the many students, friends, and family who have filled my life and challenged my ideas. Thousands of students at Wichita State University have asked questions, inserted comments, argued, fought, pushed, prodded, and said the most profound and foolish things. They have also created in me a wonderful optimism for the future. If there is some hope for this earth, it lies with their generation.

The people of New Creation Fellowship Church in Newton, Kansas have done so much to be the body of Christ for me and for our community. It is through our mutual struggles, failures, and honesty that I see glimpse of what the church could be.

Many people have read and commented on sections of this book. The beer-and-theology group that met at *Reba's* on Thursdays has contributed by reading and commenting on chunks of this book, but more by being constant partners throughout the years. Thanks also to Caleb Lázaro Moreno for his encouragement, comments, and suggestions, and to my son John for believing that I have something to say to his generation. Chris and Christine Crouse-Dyck read the whole thing and made many helpful suggestions and criticisms. Parts of my extended family have also read it, then mostly smiled and shook their heads. Yeah, thanks.

Thanks to the baristas at *Mojo's* coffee shop for friendly smiles and great tea. Additional thanks to the creators of OpenOffice who allowed me to write without needing to wrestle with Word.

Obviously the foolishness that follows is something I can take little credit for. Scholars reading this will recognize the ideas of many others. Originality, after all, is just a matter of forgetting where you read something. "We see so far because we sit on the heads of giants" (or something like that). Of the hundreds of scholars who have contributed to this, two deserve special mention. David Jobling and Brian Peckham continued to point me back to the text, to the Bible as it is rather than the Bible as I

Acknowledgments

wanted it to be. Numerous times while writing I heard their laughter in the back of my mind.

The real birthplace of this book was a discussion with a group of high school youth at a graduation party. Their responses and questions are the foundation for what follows. So thanks Sarah, Martin, Erin, Laurel, Ardys, Chloe, and Neil. I hope that what follows can be part of the vision and energy you bring to the church.

1

Introduction

DOES THE CHURCH HAVE anything to offer this world? Every day the news is filled with challenges facing the planet and the human race: overpopulation, increasing income inequality, climate change, and a wide range of other issues. We are facing problems that were unimaginable even a generation ago. If the church claims to offer "salvation" to the world, how is this a response to the threats facing life on earth?

The question remains the same when we look at more personal problems. Does the church have anything to offer a person faced with depression, a family in breakdown, or people faced with poverty, disease, and hunger? Does the church have something to offer besides band-aid fixes—individual solutions to systemic problems?

Most people inside the church will likely answer yes to these questions. This yes, however, may be more hopeful than substantial. Inside the church, we like to think we have "the answer," and we believe this answer covers a wide range of questions. What is often lacking is a clear sense of what the answer actually is and how that answer arises out of who we are as a church. This book is offered to those who are looking for the resources necessary to find that answer. It is for those inside the church who believe the church is part of a solution. It is also for those outside the church who still have some hope for the church and are waiting for signs that the church is connected to the real world. My goal is to provide some solid reflection on the Bible and its role in finding a way forward for our world.

I want to warn you, however, that you may not like some of these reflections. If you are hoping for a series of Bible verses that lead to a single, simple answer to the world's problems, you are going to be disappointed.

You Are Not Going to Heaven (and why it doesn't matter)

There is no *single* answer to the wide range of problems we face, and the problems facing societies and individuals today are much too complex for any *simple* answer. Often churches offer no answers at all but instead seems content to stick its head in the sand and hope the problems go away. So if you want a book that gives simple religious answers to complex social/economic/political questions, there are lots of those available already, but this is not one.

On the other hand, if you are looking for an honest discussion on both the good news and the bad news found in the Bible, then this book is for you. If you've looked ahead to the chapter titles, you may have been surprised to see that there is both good news and bad news in both testaments. Christians are more likely to expect either all good news, or else expect the Old Testament to supply the bad news and the New Testament to save the day. That approach is fine if you don't really want to get into significant details or generally take the Bible seriously. It is also the approach of many pastors and theologians because it provides an easy, singular foundation for belief. This idea of a Bible with a single core message is comforting, especially in a postmodern, post-Christian world that claims all truth as contextual and partial.

This kind of discussion happens all the time in my university classes. For example, in studying the Gospel of Luke, we discover that Luke makes no connection between the death of Jesus and the forgiveness of sin. This comes as a shock to some of the students, who have been raised to believe that the central message of the New Testament is that Jesus died so that their sins could be forgiven. What they find is that the gospels present different ideas of what the "central message" of the Jesus event is. So as readers of the Bible, we must choose among various visions of who Jesus was.

Most people want to find a single, clear destination and route for their spiritual journey. But I can't honestly proclaim any single core message because the Bible does not have one. One of the consequences of having four Gospels in the New Testament (rather than just one) is that we must recognize that the truth is neither simple nor singular. Our understanding of the message of Jesus is filtered in four different ways in the Gospels and further filtered by our own consciousness. If we then add the rest of the Bible to this discussion, the results become more rather than less complex.

Instead, the Bible provides a wide range of ideas and principles, thought systems and theologies. Many of these are mutually exclusive. In fact, much of the Bible is none of these but includes stories of events and

Introduction

characters, some of which are disturbing or horrifying. Part of being honest with the Bible is a willingness to say no to some parts of it. The Bible is itself a series of arguments about who God really is and how the world was created to work. Any attempt to make sense of the Bible involves choosing among the options presented.

This is often shocking to my students, yet it is a fairly standard part of biblical scholarship. People in the church talk about "the message of the Bible," but scholarship distinguishes between Paul and Matthew's views on the Jewish law, between the Gospel of John and Revelation on the end of the world, and even between the various "Pauls" we encounter when we study his letters carefully. One of the difficulties I find in teaching New Testament courses is to keep remembering that these ideas, which I have come to regard as obvious, are often disturbing to my students.

Our task as readers is to choose and act. If we pretend to believe it all, we are being intellectually dishonest and we're stuck with a whole range of contradictory responses to any situation. Do we love our enemies or enact genocide? Do we treat the world around us as hell-bound sinners or sheep without a shepherd? Is God's character primarily founded on love or on power? If we refuse to decide, we end up with libraries full of twisted argumentation about minutia rather than lives full of healing. Trying to say everything, we end up saying nothing. This is not the way forward.

The need to choose is part of the good news. People do not need to be squeezed into one-size-fits-all boxes to be the faithful children of God. The way forward for this earth and for the church is not one where everyone does the same thing for the same reason. The Bible recognizes and celebrates this. This book also celebrates this, while also recognizing that many of the paths chosen by the church are not helpful in bringing salvation. There are many wrong answers to the question of defining "salvation." Having multiple options is different from "anything goes."

This way of understanding the Bible may challenge ideas about the Bible held both inside and outside the church. The intent in reading the Bible in this way is not to challenge the authority of the Bible but to challenge the church to read the Bible it has, rather than the Bible it wishes it had. The Bible has stood as a sure foundation for faith for the past 2,000 years, so is unlikely to be threatened by any comments made about it here. In fact, attempts at sugar coating the contents of the Bible are likely to do more harm than good, especially in a study that is trying to be honest about the consequences of the Christian life in the real world. If we can't be honest about what the Bible says, it is unlikely we will succeed in being honest about much else.

The final answer to the question Does the church have anything to offer? will be, I hope so. While in theory the answer should be yes, in practice too often the answer is no. As Christians, we need to choose.

On the other hand, most people outside the church will answer no to these questions. Many have given up on the church. Others have never seen any answer coming from the church that attracts them or provides real answers to their questions and problems. If you are one of these people, this book is meant to encourage you not to give up on the church. I hope to convince you that the church can be part of the solution and that we can work together.

There is no point pretending that the church has all the answers. The Bible says nothing directly about groundwater pollution or Internet privacy or making prescriptions more affordable. So the question is not whether the church has all the answers. It doesn't. The goal here is humbler. I want to explore what, if anything, we have to contribute.

As someone inside the church, I also need to begin with confession. The church too often is part of the problem. Either the gospel has been captured by those who benefit from the status quo, or churches only offer escape. Sometimes it seems the church is deliberately trying to become the opiate of the masses while preaching comfort to the comfortable. So the church is the first to promote militarism and colonialism, defend torture, condemn homosexuals, and deny our responsibility for climate change. Too often the church appears to be proclaiming salvation while promoting destruction and division.

Somehow, then, the church needs to find a way of proclaiming the gospel boldly but humbly. We need to proclaim with our ears and hands, rather than with our mouths and multimedia presentations. When we are ready to listen first, work second, and proclaim third, we may regain some credibility in the larger effort to find a way forward for this earth.

SALVATION

So if we ask What does the church have to offer this world? the answer is usually, Salvation. Salvation is a good religious word. Part of Christian education is learning how and when to use it, without worrying about what

Introduction

it actually means. It sits alongside words such as *faith* and *righteousness* and *blessing* as words you need to know how to use to sound properly religious.

But what happens when we try to figure out what salvation actually means? In looking around for that answer, I have been surprised at how difficult it is to find a good, solid answer. Usually the discussions that follow the question of salvation center around "atonement." Atonement is about how to get salvation or how salvation is given (and which of these is the better wording). Other discussions center around how you can know (or not know) whether you have salvation. Not much discussion is about what salvation actually is.

To put it another way, atonement is about how we get there. Salvation is about where we are going. Stated this way, it is rather odd to expend a lot of effort charting the directions if we have not yet defined our goal. Google Maps cannot help us find directions if we can't state our destination. So this book is about destinations. It is about what the church is offering people when it offers salvation.

Part of the problem is that inside the church, salvation is thought of as a "religious" word. It is about spiritual stuff, about souls and heaven and things beyond. If this is the context for salvation, and if salvation is the heart of the gospel message, then the answer to our initial question is rather simple. If the church's response to the huge problems facing the earth is to offer it a fully spiritualized salvation, then the church has nothing substantial to offer the world. At best we are offering cream pie to a world hungry for life-giving food. At worst we are offering pictures of food or promises of food, answers that pretend the problems are not real, and we only mock the suffering of the world around us.

What follows is an attempt to think about salvation as a lived experience. That is, I want to start by asking the question, What do we expect to happen (or not happen) *here, on this earth*, as a result of salvation? If salvation has no consequences for our world, then it is a rather safe but benign idea that we can discuss (or not) for hours over coffee without really worrying about our ideas being subject to verification. After all, if salvation makes no difference in the world around us, we can never be proven wrong in our contention that salvation has or has not happened.

One way to check any understanding of salvation to see if it is grounded in the real world is to think about mosquitoes. True salvation includes mosquitoes. Sometimes it may mean salvation from mosquitoes, but mostly it includes the salvation of mosquitoes. Insects are an important and necessary part of life on earth, even the ones that bite us. So as you continue to ponder the idea of salvation, watch for the impact on mosquitoes.

If we truly expect salvation to change something in the world around us, then it may be helpful to try to figure out what that change should be. We also need to understand our responsibility in this process. Are there things we can do to make these changes more readily apparent? Are there things we are doing to keep this change from actually happening? Or is the whole process completely automatic, so that as pastors and scholars we can safely wash our hands of the whole affair, and as Christians we can safely assume that "it" has happened, whatever "it" is?

My contention is that if salvation has no consequences (for us and for mosquitoes) then it isn't salvation, it's just theology. We can file it under "things to teach in church" without worrying about it further. The church, then, has no responsibility except to exist or possibly to grow. It offers salvation, and assures people that it alone can give them that, without worrying about defining this term too carefully or being responsible for anything other than the souls of individuals.

In this scenario, the task of the church is persuasion. First we need to convince people that they have souls. Then we need to convince people that their souls will survive death and will be eternally punished unless they are given the salvation offered by (and only by?) the church. This is certainly a large task and one that is becoming increasingly difficult in a post-Christian world. It is also a task that has little connection to the social, political, and economic reality around us.

Few churches actually subscribe completely to such a purely ahistorical view of salvation. But parts of this view often inhabit parts of most churches and affect how churches sees themselves and their mission. This is especially true in the absence of any alternative definition. So if the church's core mission is to proclaim the message of salvation, how does this connect to the other parts of the church's mission? Are there concrete markers (besides church growth) that demonstrate whether or not this salvation is happening? If this salvation comes from God, are there signs in the world around us that God is doing that (whatever "that" is)?

This is part of the larger question of whether Christians today really expect God to act in the world beyond the "spiritual" level. Many people talk about Jesus in their hearts, but do they also expect to see God acting in the world around them? After all, if God does not act beyond the personal, spiritual realm, then the church really has nothing to say to the larger problems of our world. Then it will hold people's hands and offer comfort and warm fuzzy feelings but will leave larger problems to politicians, generals, and scientists. So is God concerned about and active in the world?

I encounter this question in a number of places in life. As I write, for example, we are in a drought here in Kansas. It isn't particularly serious, but we could certainly use some more rain. The weather experts say this drought is partially caused by the water temperature in the Pacific, as well as other, less clear causes from global climate change. This sounds like a reasonable explanation. I believe in cause and effect and see little reason to disagree with people who have spent their lives trying to understand this particular system.

On the other hand, I also believe God can bring rain. This is not to say God automatically brings rain when we humans ask for it. But when we pray for rain, I don't think we are doing something inherently ignorant or foolish. Yet I wonder if that is true for most Christians around me. I wonder this because I have on occasion suggested that churches get together to hold prayer services for rain and have not had any positive responses. Maybe I have been talking to the wrong people, or maybe I haven't said it loudly enough, but no one else has organized such a service either.

So, getting back to salvation, do most Christians operate with a consciousness that expects God to respond to us, either positively or negatively, beyond the "spiritual" level? Many people do feel/think/believe/know that God works in the hearts of people, that God cares for people's souls or spirits, that at some deeper level God continues to act in the world. But does God move out of God's appointed realm and interact with larger natural or human systems?

Part of the issue here is the compartmentalization of life that happens naturally in modern societies. We live our lives in ways that result in a worldview in which each thing has its own realm of influence. As parents, our influence is largely limited to our families. At work, we encounter different people and have different responsibilities and tasks. Our church often represents a different group of people and a different sphere of influence. So, despite the attempts by the pastor to tell us that God is interested and involved in the whole of our existence, it is natural that we relegate God's influence to the "spiritual" world, linked to "church stuff" more readily than home stuff or work stuff or the natural cycles of the world around us.

A second part of the issue is the loss of the God of negative consequences. Do Christians still believe in a God of punishment, or does God only give or withhold blessings? For example, last semester there was a student in my New Testament course who was of Buddhist background. Toward the end of the course, when we were studying the book of Revelation, I asked students to respond emotionally to the book. How did it make them feel? This Buddhist student said that it made her afraid. I responded by suggesting that surely she was not afraid of God. She responded that yes, she was definitely afraid of God, now that she had taken this course. This was surprising, given that I teach about the God of love found in the Bible. But then I realized that the New Testament, while saying much about this God of love, also contains many verses about God's wrath on those outside the Christian community (e.g. Matthew 3:7, Romans 1:18, John 3:16–18). So my reading of the New Testament was an insider's reading, but an outsider like this Buddhist student had been told regularly that God's punishment awaits her at some point in the future.

Here is the most obvious place where salvation has major consequences in the New Testament. The lack of salvation leads to God's wrath when Jesus returns. The problem is that, 2,000 years after Jesus' death, and after hundreds of failed attempts to predict his return, it is increasingly difficult to credibly proclaim that Jesus will return in the near future. And if we refuse to shift the consequences of sin completely to hellfire in the afterlife (for reasons discussed later), what reason do we have to fear God's wrath? There is, of course, still the possibility that God's positive actions (blessings) will be withheld from us if salvation does not happen. In this way, the lack of positive consequences still makes salvation meaningful, so neither hellfire nor apocalyptic expectation are a necessary part of a theology of salvation. But as I said, salvation without consequences is just theology.

On the other hand, *what if God really does have a will and plan for this earth*? What if God is just as (or more) concerned with political and economic systems as with individual souls? What if the spiritual world is so connected to social and military systems as to be inseparable? If so, then salvation is something that happens on this earth. Then salvation is a process whose progress can be measured. If this is so, does the church have a responsibility in bringing the message *and the actions* of salvation to the world around us? And what must be said to a church that is more often part of the problem than part of the solution for a suffering world?

In order to provide an answer for these sorts of questions, we are going to look to the Bible while also focusing on human experience. I look to the Bible because that's what I do—I teach and preach the Bible for a living.

That's my training and my passion. The Bible also gives those of us in the church a common story and vocabulary for thinking about the world we live in. We look to lived experience because it is unavoidable. All thinking is filtered through the lenses of language and experience, so we might as well do this honestly, as well as we are able.

We will be using the Bible as a guide, not an answer book. Or rather, we will see in the Bible a number of different answers to the question of a way forward. Some of the answers found in the Bible are going to be rejected. Partly this is because, as I said earlier, some parts of the Bible reject other parts, and we need to choose.

More often, however, we are going to reject parts of the Bible because of our focus on human experience. The issue is not whether the Bible conforms to our experiences. The question we are going to ask is whether Bible writers took their own experiences seriously, and then see how they responded to them. Occasionally we are going to see that the Bible is a denial of the experiences of God that the writers had. That is, sometimes the writers experienced God in a certain way, yet wrote something else. When this is true, we need to learn from their experiences, not from their writings.

Thinking about human experience is an incredibly difficult thing in itself. What are the limits of things that count as "real experiences"? After all, dreams are experiences; reading fantasy books is an experience. You might talk to someone and experience their anger, only to find out later that they weren't really angry. This entire episode is an experience. Your experience of misunderstanding their anger is still an experience.

In this context, we are going to think about experience as a broad category. It includes things we have seen, but also things we have read, stories we have heard, our own belief/disbelief, our experiences of God and those of others. Reading the Bible is part of our experience, whether or not we believe or understand what it says.

The Bible has proven to be a sure foundation for the church. In it we read many experiences that are beyond our own. Things happened to Moses, to Peter, and to the woman at the well that have not happened to us. These stories are part of how God works. Perhaps we can expect God to act in similar ways for us. So one of the questions we need to ask is whether the biblical account is based on the actual experiences of those writing it. The answer (spoiler alert) is both yes and no for both testaments. The writers of the Bible were just as capable of denying reality as we are. Often our ideas of "the God we want" overpower our experiences of the God who is. So we write and preach about the way we wish God acted.

These experiences also allow us to make sense of the world around us. They create expectations for the future. We learn to distinguish between the expected (things fall down when we drop them) and the unexpected (you say "good morning" to a friend, and she slaps your face) and the impossible (you pet your dog, and she turns into a balloon).

I would like to apply this idea to the spiritual world. If we perform a certain action toward God, what do we expect to happen? Do we actually expect God to act in any situation, and if so, when and how? Do we expect mountains to move when we tell them to, or healing to happen when we pray for it? In regard to salvation, if salvation "happens," what do we expect has happened or will happen? Are there other things that will happen as a result of this?

A problem comes when our expectations overwhelm our experiences. If we expect something and it absolutely fails to happen, what do we do? This is especially true when it comes to the actions of God. If we expect blessings and instead experience one bad thing after another, how do we respond? If we believe in God as a loving presence and find God to be consistently absent or apparently uncaring, what do we do? These sorts of things happened to some of the writers of the Bible. Their responses are recorded for us to read. Sometimes their expectations so overwhelmed their experiences that they told stories of the God they wanted, rather than the God they got.

My contention in this book is that we need to deal with the God who exists rather than the one of our fantasies. I believe that human experiences of God provide the best picture of who God really is. But I also believe that sometimes desire overwhelms reality. When this happens, we should not use our desire as a guide for the way forward. This is just as true for theology as it is for physics. If you drop a ball, ultimately it doesn't matter whether you were expecting God to keep it from falling or you were wanting gravity to make an exception for you, the ball is still going to fall. And if you dump poisonous chemicals into the groundwater and expect to draw clean water from the well, you have little reason to expect God to have miraculously removed the chemicals unless you have experiences that confirm this as a possibility.

This is especially important when we think about salvation. Ideas about salvation so easily become rescue fantasies. We want a God who will

Introduction

descend from heaven and solve all our problems. This is a natural extension of the desire for someone who will do this for us. We need a millionaire uncle who will pay all our debts, a superman who will rescue us from the bad guys, and a superpill that will make all our problems go away. These fantasies are natural.

Yet it does not take a lot of living in the world to realize how often these things fail to happen. The millionaire uncle remains mysteriously absent. The bad guys show up, but Superman doesn't. The superpill fixes some problems but is expensive, has side effects, and doesn't change the underlying condition. And God utterly fails to rain fire and brimstone on our enemies.

So then we need to choose how to respond. We can continue to live in a fantasy. Much of the entertainment industry is based on rescue fantasies. The church often picks up this theme and offers weekly spiritual rescue fantasies to those in the pews (or the new comfortable theater seating). Or we can take an honest look at the world around us and at our experiences of the God who is and try to find a way forward for the human race.

I believe God is a necessary and important part of this way forward. I also believe that many of the people who will walk with me on this journey disagree about the existence or nature of God. I also realize, sadly, that too often Christians will be working against fellow Christians who either prefer the fantasy or have a very different vision of the way forward. This book is an attempt to increase the number of Christians and churches who will work together toward the goal of the salvation of the earth. It is also an attempt to increase the number of non-Christians who believe that the church can be part of the solution, rather than only part of the problem.

In the chapters that follow, I hope to present ideas that both encourage and disturb you. Chapters 2 and 3 will likely be the most disturbing. You may be tempted to skip them and get on to the "good news" in the remaining chapters. I encourage you not to do this. This is like skipping Good Friday and just showing up for Easter. This, again, is the God we want, backed up by the Bible we want. And it is a fantasy. If you aren't ready for chapters 2 and 3, then you aren't ready for the good news.

The remaining chapters outline the resources from the Bible and the church that can contribute to the larger project of salvation. They are offered to you so that you can offer them to others. They are offered in a spirit of humility and honesty, the two most important virtues the church today can cultivate. Think of them as extensions of the statement, "I'd like to help;

11

here's what I bring." I have no illusions that salvation can only happen inside the church. My hope is that *some* salvation can happen inside the church.

This is my initial statement. I look forward to many responses so that this monologue can become a conversation. Even more, I look forward to hearing about how this monologue has contributed to salvation. The purpose of this book is to encourage salvation to happen, rather than just encourage discussion about salvation.

GOING TO HEAVEN?

For many people, this is the major question about which Christianity, and even religion in general, is concerned. This is true both inside and outside the church. Most Americans believe that some part of themselves will survive their death, and they turn to religion to help them solve the question of what will happen to their eternal soul. For most of my students, this is the focus of the definition of salvation: people who are "saved" go to heaven, and the rest don't.

Obviously I really have no idea whether or not you are going to heaven. Even if I did, there is little reason for you to believe me. But I firmly believe that it doesn't matter, and in fact, if you are really concerned about the answer to this question, the answer is probably no.

The answer is no for a number of reasons. The first one is simple logic. If you ask most people what it takes to get into heaven, their answer will likely have something to do with faith. The logic here is simple.[1] If you believe that getting to heaven is the result of being saved, then when you read the Bible you will see that the New Testament regularly links salvation and something called faith. There is certainly some discussion in the New Testament about the nature of the relationship between salvation and faith, but the two ideas are often linked. So if faith is necessary for salvation, and salvation leads to going to heaven, then logically faith is what gets you into heaven.

At this point, it may be helpful to define "faith." While my students usually start by equating faith and *belief* (simple mental assent to an idea), more thorough study will also add ideas like *loyalty* and *trust* to the definition. This makes sense when you think about it, because part of the issue with faith is that you need to trust that God will do what God has promised (namely have a heaven ready for those who are saved).

1. And wrong, but we'll get to that later.

Introduction

So here is where it gets tricky. If you need to have faith to get to heaven, and if trust is a significant part of faith, then it follows that someone who asks the question Am I going to heaven? does not trust, therefore does not have faith, and therefore is not going to heaven. This means that the act of asking the question already answers the question in the negative. If you ask, the answer is no.

This is one reason it doesn't matter. Either you trust God, in which case the question doesn't matter, or you don't, in which case you know you're not. Besides, if God is not trustworthy, then it really doesn't matter at all. You can have faith or not, be good or not, save the world or not, and an untrustworthy God may or may not respond as promised.

The much more important reason why it doesn't matter whether you are going to heaven is that "going to heaven" is not a significant part of a biblical understanding of "salvation." This is not to say that it doesn't exist as part of the answer to what salvation is, but it isn't a major part.

Take the Gospel of John as an example. The Gospel of John has 879 verses. Of these, only two are directly about life after death (14:2, 3, "In my Father's house there are many dwelling places . . ."), and these verses are directly preceded by 14:1, "Do not let your hearts be troubled. Believe in God, believe also in me." So the only two verses in John directly about going to heaven are preceded by an encouragement not to worry about it. While John's Gospel does contain many instances of the phrase "eternal life," this phrase is about life before death rather than life after death.

So the most straightforward reading of John's Gospel says there are 877 verses about something other than life after death, and two about going to heaven (assuming for the moment that Jesus is talking about heaven in these verses). If this ratio is an indication of priorities, then concerns about heaven should only occupy two-tenths of 1 percent of a Christian faith.

Thus, the second reason it doesn't matter is because the Bible says it doesn't matter and in fact warns against worrying about it ("Do not let your hearts be troubled"). So if it matters to you, then you are not paying sufficient attention to the Bible (assuming that you think the Bible is a reliable guide to the Christian faith). And, in the Christian scheme of things, not paying attention to the Bible is going to hinder your chances of getting to heaven.

In what follows, we want to continue to focus on three things. The first is to take a real, honest look at what the Bible says and does not say. We want to read the Bible-we-have, rather than finding the bits that fit into the Bible-we-want. In doing this, we will especially note places where the writers of the Bible do not seem to deal with the reality of the world around them. These will form the "bad news" sections of this book. Fortunately not all the news is bad, and we will also see that the Bible-we-have still contains much good news for ourselves and our world.

The second focus is to be as honest as we can about how we see God working in the world. I use the word "see" here not only as a metaphor for "understand," but also literally. Where do you *see* God at work? What *kinds* of things does God do? What kinds of things do we want God to do that God doesn't do? This final question will form part of our search for a more honest understanding of God. Just as we will read the Bible-we-have, we also want to be honest about the God-we-have, rather than waiting for the God-we-want.

The final focus is to take an honest look at the world around us and try to figure out if the Bible is a helpful partner in the continuation of human life on earth and in the improvement of the quality of that life. If we take heaven out of the picture, then salvation is something that happens here on earth. What then is this message of salvation, and how does it affect our lives on earth? If we can answer this question, then we should be better prepared to confront the challenges ahead, whatever they may be.

The theme we are *not* going to focus on is heaven. Heaven doesn't matter. God will take care of heaven; our task is to take care of the earth. What will happen after you die? Life will continue here on earth without you. Someone may need to clean up the mess you left behind. Someone else may benefit from the good you did. That much you know for sure. The God-we-have will be able to take things from there without your help.

2

Old Testament—the bad news

WHY BAD NEWS?

THE TASK OF THE church is to proclaim the good news (the meaning of *gospel*) of salvation. Thus, most books on salvation focus entirely on the good news and find that good news in various parts of the Bible. In doing this, they simply ignore the parts of the Bible that do not fit their idea of what constitutes "good news." They also regularly fail to explain how they distinguish between good news and bad news inside the Bible. In contrast, I want to be more open about the bad news sections. I also want to explain how to decide what is good news and what is bad. As stated in the introduction, this book is an attempt to ground the idea of salvation in human experience. Human experience will also be the guide for interacting with the Bible as we search for this good news.

Much of the Bible is the record of God's interaction with human beings. As people experienced the presence or absence of God, they wrote of these events and reflected on them. There are parts of the Bible, however, where the writers appear to be writing in contradiction to their experiences. That is, they experienced God working in one way, but wrote about God working in a really different way. Insofar as we can distinguish between these true and false reflections on the actions of God, we will use this as the way of deciding between good news and bad.

When the writers of the Bible wrote things that contradicted their experience, they usually wrote about the God they wanted rather than the

God they had. They were hoping for grand rescues, heroes indisputably appointed by God to fix their problems, or clear direction from God when none was forthcoming. They wanted a big, flashy God who would ride in on a white stallion and show the world that they were right. So they wrote stories of the "good old days" or the "wonderful future God has promised." Rather than acknowledging the salvation they had experienced (which was often much less than ideal), they wrote about the salvation they wanted.

Now hope is a powerful thing. So are grand stories about the past. Both of these are important for many people in a wide variety of situations. There are good reasons why the writers of the Bible included many stories about "the good old days" and "the time when God rescued us." These became some of the best-loved stories in the Bible. They also included stories about the future, which formed the basis for struggle against oppression and hatred.

The problem arises today when we attempt to base our current plans on the expectation that God will continue to act in these great and obvious ways. If these stories are not grounded in the actual events of the writer's experience, they will not provide an accurate picture on which to base current expectations. For example, imagine that you have taken out a loan with the bank and then lost your job. Your bank manager then lowers your payments for a few months, in order to help you stay current with your account. Now imagine that, instead of telling your children this story, you tell them that the bank manager forgave your entire loan and you further imply that this is how bank managers usually operate. This may lead to a situation where your children have wildly incorrect expectations regarding the forgiveness of bank loans and the risks involved in borrowing money.

The same is true for the actions of God. If we plan for the future based on stories that did not arise from the actual experiences of the biblical writers, we may end up expecting actions from God that are wildly unrealistic. If we do something dramatic in confronting the government of a particular country and expect God to rescue us miraculously from the consequences of our actions, we need either to be sure that God will show up as expected or we need to have a backup plan.

METHOD

One of the most significant transformations in biblical studies today is the turn away from an "innocent" reading of the text. Traditionally, the Bible

Old Testament—the bad news

is read as a description of its surface contents— that the story of the Exodus should be read as a story about an event in which slaves escaped from Egypt, and that other stories should be read in similar ways. This is still the mainstay of biblical scholarship and one of the reasons few pay attention to what biblical scholarship says. So long as the argument is simply about events long ago, most people have little reason to think they should care.

More recently, from a whole variety of perspectives, attention has turned toward what the Bible does, or rather what was or is done with the Bible. A complete description and analysis of this movement is beyond the scope of this book. Briefly, within the context of this study, however, I will start with the understanding that, while history is about the past, history writing is equally about the present. That is, the way people write history can tell us just as much about the realities of the writer and audience as it does about the actual subject of the writing. So the focus question will be: *Why are these people writing this story in this way at this time?*

To illustrate how this question works, think about a modern American history textbook you might find in a typical high school classroom. The book will be about major events in American history that happened long ago. But the choice of stories, the way they are told, and the pictures that may be included all will tell us much about the perspective and concerns of the authors. So one textbook might highlight the Vietnam War as a significant lesson in American foreign policy, while another textbook might not mention the war at all, preferring only to talk about American victories. In this way, the textbook tells us both something about events in the past (what happened) and the concerns of the present (what current American foreign policy should be). The same is true of the Bible. Its stories tell us about events of the past and the concerns of the authors. In this book, we will focus on the second question.

As I stated in the introduction, this study is centered on the question, What do we expect to happen (or not happen) as a result of salvation? These expectations are to some extent based on experience, either our own or those of others. For Christians and Jews, these experiences include those found in the Old Testament. These texts are read as part of the larger community experience and therefore as a guide to what might happen in the present and in the future. If God is the same "yesterday, today and forever," then the stories in the Bible provide examples of how God works. If God did something in the past, there is no particular reason to believe God will not do it again.

You Are Not Going to Heaven (and why it doesn't matter)

So what experiences does the Old Testament draw on for its presentation of the way God works in the world? If we look at the stories that are drawn upon to tell the story of "Israel," and as we look at the outcome of the telling of these stories, what do we learn about what the "people of Israel" might have actually expected to happen when "salvation" happened? This will be a guide for us as we think about what our salvation might look like.

EXODUS

Much work on the "biblical idea of salvation" starts in or around Exodus. The people of Israel were slaves in Egypt, far from the promised land, oppressed and hungry (Exodus 1). The story then recounts the many actions of God in freeing them from slavery. God brought Moses out of the wilderness to confront Pharaoh and lead the people (Exodus 3). God turned Aaron's rod into a snake (7:8–13). God brought the ten plagues (7:14—11:10). God provided the cloud by day and fiery pillar by night (13:20-22). God opened up a way in the Red Sea (14). God provided manna and quail in the desert (16). God promised to drive out the Canaanites (and probably also the mosquitoes) when they got to the promised land (33:2). The people themselves were largely passive, needing only to follow, herded like sheep from Egypt to Sinai and on. They only needed to follow the Great Shepherd, and he would take care of all their problems.

This Exodus paradigm, then, is the basis for much thinking and writing about who God is and how God acts in history. This discussion, as well as countless debates about the historical basis for the Exodus story, assumes that the Exodus story is primarily concerned with the events it relates, as well as the interpretation of these events by later peoples.

Read in another light, however, the story of the Exodus is not about slaves fleeing Egypt. The question I suggested earlier for this study was, Why do these people write this story in this way at this time? So we need to slow down and fill in some of the parts of the question before we can continue our study of Exodus.

The story of Exodus is part of the Torah, the first five books of the Bible. This story itself is not a complete story, ending as it does on the borders of the "promised land." The story only reaches its conclusion at the end of 2 Kings, with the exile of the leadership of Israel to Babylon. This larger story (Genesis—2 Kings) we are going to call the Grand Narrative. It is the story of the people of Israel from creation (Genesis) through the fall of Jerusalem in 587 BC (2 Kings), encompassing the whole history of the people to that point. It forms much of the basis for the identity of the people of Israel, as it sets down the entire history of the universe as it relates to a specific people. While constructed in stages from the works of a variety of authors and editors, it relates a continuous story of a people and their God.

Since history is always written after the event, we need to assume that the Grand Narrative reaches its current form sometime after the Israelites are taken into captivity in Babylon. It certainly contains many older traditions and stories that may have been included in the Grand Narrative without significant editing. Speculation on these matters takes up large sections of many libraries and shows few signs of slowing.

One of the results of these studies is the notion that the Grand Narrative itself contains a variety of points of view. It is one story but a story that reflects an ongoing debate about the past, present, and future of the people of Israel. There are parts of the story that see no future *without* a monarchy, and other parts that see no future *for* the monarchy. Some parts give important roles to prophets, while other parts see prophets as grouchy old men who want to hold on to power.

Another important question is *when*. When does the Grand Narrative attain its current shape and character? There is no simple answer to this question, since the current shape of the Grand Narrative is more a result of process than event. There were undoubtedly earlier versions, bits and pieces added in at various times by various editors, and probably no single version that everyone was working from. Even a reasonable description of the process involves much speculation and many thousands of words. Regularly the discussion of the process takes so much time that people do not get around to actually reading the text to see what it says.

For the purposes of this study, I am going to presume that the Grand Narrative reflects the ongoing debate within the community of "Israel" during the Persian period (roughly 520—330 BC). It may be that some of the people involved in the process lived in Babylon or Egypt (or points between), but mostly we are going to focus on the text as reflecting the perspective of those who had returned from Babylon and were living in or around Jerusalem while still under Persian rule.

So while the stories of Exodus are "about" the "people of Israel" who came out of Egypt, a story placed within history somewhere around 1200 BC, they are equally "about" the constitution of the "people of Israel" who have came of Babylon to claim ownership of the city of Jerusalem and its immediate environs (roughly 450 BC).[1] The exodus and the Grand Narrative provided the ideological foundation for a certain group of people and their claim to a specific geographical area. So what happens to our understanding of salvation if we read the Grand Narrative as a product of the Persian period? What real-world consequences did this story have for them?

After the "return from Exile" (in quotes because this designation itself is part of the story), these people claimed as their founding identity the story of the Exodus. They were the people of the God "who brought you out of the land of Egypt" (a repeated phrase in Exodus, Leviticus, and Deuteronomy). They recorded and celebrated this event while not actually recording significant details regarding the journey from Babylon to Jerusalem. In fact, the Bible records nothing about the actual journey to or from Babylon. After a journey of hundreds of miles through what must have been a host of challenging circumstances, these people instead chose to tell the story of a much earlier journey to that land, the Exodus from Egypt. They had just experienced their own exodus but preferred to write about another one, one that happened hundreds of years earlier.

And wouldn't you? "We walked hundreds of miles" hardly makes for a grand narrative of identity. We can presume that the journey out of Babylonian captivity was accomplished without significant acts of divine intervention. If the people journeying from Babylon to Judea were fed with manna or led by a fiery pillar, they presumably would have recorded this. Instead they were silent about this journey, just as God appears to have been silent during the journey. Rather, they celebrate the Exodus, the event in which God did the things that gods are supposed to do. The Exodus story connected them to "the God who acts in history." Their claim to be the true people of this God and their understanding of this God was based not on the actions of God that they had witnessed in their own exodus from Babylon but on a story that stood in stark contrast to their actual experiences.

Imagine that a friend of yours goes on an extended vacation, one she has been dreaming about for many years. Upon her return, you get together to hear all the stories and see the (too) many pictures. Yet when you see her, she pulls out a dusty photo album and starts to tell you about a trip her grandmother took many years ago. Likely you would conclude that her vacation did not live up to her expectations. This is what the people of Israel

---

1. It is important to remember that the identity of the "people of Israel" is itself a construction of the Grand Narrative. The question Who are we? and the parallel question Who is not part of us? is answered through story rather than through DNA evidence.

did after their journey from exile back to Jerusalem. They told the stories from hundreds of years ago, rather than the stories of their own journey.

This means that the identity of Israel is based not within living memory but in the hoary mists of time. In significant ways, the story of the Exodus is both the story of the God who acted (in the exodus from Egypt) and the story of the God who failed to act (in the exodus from Babylon). Telling the first story without recounting the second results in a history that chose not to tell about the real experiences of these people. This description of the (in)action of God also applies to the Law. The instructions of God were not given by the God who miraculously delivered them out of Babylon but by the One who (presumably) gave the Law and then failed to show up for the long walk from Babylon to Jerusalem. So in speaking about salvation, we need to recognize that the salvation offered in the Law is clearly disconnected from the actions of this God in the living memory of those who composed the story as we now have it.

Yet paradoxically, one of the results of adopting the Exodus story as a narrative of origins is that the Exodus becomes a paradigm for how God works. This can easily be demonstrated by the hundreds of uses to which the Exodus has been put in history and in theology. Scholars, preachers, and rabbis throughout history have looked to the Exodus as the story that provides the foundation for an understanding of who God is and how God works. "See," they say, pointing to the Exodus story, "*that* is how our God acts."

The problem with using the Exodus story as a paradigm is that it doesn't get repeated as a regular pattern. While the crossing of the Red Sea gets repeated in the crossing of the Jordan in Joshua 3, and later by the crossings of the Jordan by Elijah and Elisha (2 Kings 2), each time it happens it becomes a smaller event. And we look in vain for further repetitions in all of history. Stories such as the ten plagues or manna in the desert or the numerous other events that make the Exodus so compelling are without parallel. In fact, it is the uniqueness of the Exodus story that makes it so significant.

The difficulty, then, is that the same story is used both for its uniqueness and for establishing a paradigm. But it doesn't work to use an exception as a paradigm. Moses, burning bush, exodus, Red Sea, manna, across the Jordan, a few (but surprisingly few) miracles to start the conquest, and then the paradigm ends, never to be repeated. From then on, Israel is mostly on its own, with the occasional flash of prophetic miracle (events that are also part of the Grand Narrative). The simple fact that all these events are recorded in the Grand Narrative of Origin, events that are placed hundreds of years before the Grand Narrative takes its current shape, suggests that these events are not ongoing for the people of Israel during the Persian period. Why tell stories of the good old days if things are better today? Those in charge of producing the official story of Israel appear to have needed the stories of long ago at least partly because these events had no parallel in their own time.

So the Exodus provided a picture of salvation based on the idea that God rescues people through grand events where the work of God is unmistakable. The plagues provided the perfect example, with further examples at the Red Sea and the many miracles along the way. The people's task in all of this was to trust that God would do what God had promised. Salvation came directly through the intervention of God, and the people were largely passive. In fact, the actions of the people recorded in the Exodus story are mostly negative. They sinned (Exodus 32:1–30), they quarreled (17:1–7), and they disobeyed (16:24–27). Passivity was thus encouraged, as the best that people could manage was to get in God's way.

All this would be a great paradigm for salvation if, in fact, it was repeated on a regular basis. The absence of further examples of this sort of direct, obvious manifestation of God's power forces us to confront the disparity between expectation and experience. If the Exodus is paradigmatic for the way God works, what has happened so that God no longer works in this way? We might be tempted to limit the idea of salvation to the spiritual realm, but the Old Testament offers us no such option. In the Old Testament, whatever else it might mean, salvation should include peace, justice, and health. If salvation has no physical consequences, then it is just a meaningless term that makes us sound properly theological. Or if the results of salvation are limited to the social or psychological, then we need to admit that we have left the realm of "theology" and are undertaking group-building exercises or contemplating personal wholeness.

On the surface, then, the Exodus story appears to be an ideal example of a story about salvation told on the basis of experience. The people of Israel experienced deliverance from slavery in Egypt, and they told this story. Read as a story told after the Exile, however, the Exodus story is a paradigm for how God *doesn't* work. The God portrayed in the Exodus story is the God of power-and-might, the God of dramatic acts of undeniable presence. Yet there is no indication that the exiles who came out of Babylon experienced anything like this. No plagues, no manna, no angels. So the God of power-and-might we find in Exodus is the God the exiles wanted rather than the God they got. The Exodus story is more about the denial of experience than a reflection on the way God brought salvation.

But what if...

In retelling the Exodus story rather than recounting the experiences they had, the writers of the Grand Narrative in the postexilic community proclaimed the God of power-and-might. This was the God who worked in obvious and earth-shaking ways. These unmistakable actions were the work of God bringing salvation to the people.

This way of presenting God led immediately to a problem. What do we do when this God fails to act in this way? This is, for the postexilic community, a very real question. Is the Exodus God simply a fantasy? And more immediately, what do we do? If we are walking through the desert and manna fails to fall from the sky, what do we do? And when we enter the promised land and God fails to cause the current inhabitants of the land to flee miraculously or just disappear, what do we do?

In thinking about how the postexilic community responded to this issue, we have two resources. The most obvious is the histories of the period, as found in Ezra and Nehemiah. In these texts, we read about things the community did when faced with the question of what to do. The other place the question is answered is in the books of Joshua and Judges. In these collections, we again see an idealized picture of what the writers wished could happen. Since we have two resources that talk about the same basic issue in different ways, we can compare them to see how the historical idealization was worked out in the policies and attitudes of the real community.

The issue at hand, then, is, What do we do when the God of Exodus fails to show up? The book of Joshua deals with that question in a straightforward manner. In many ways, the answer was already foreshadowed earlier in the Grand Narrative. The largely passive role given to the people of Israel in the Exodus (they just had to be ready to leave) is soon replaced by a much more active role. When they encountered Sihon king of Heshbon, they took up arms and fought (Numbers 21:21–31). The actions of God are not mentioned in the battle account. The lesson here, then, is that if God fails to show up, we need to be ready to fight and kill.

What is additionally interesting about this particular story is the ballad sung about the battle, as recorded in Numbers 21:27–30. In the ballad, fire comes out of the cities and devours the enemy army. Although it is not clearly stated, the only reasonable explanation for the fire is God acting on behalf of Israel. Yet this fire is not mentioned in the battle account in 21:24. So here the text appears to be telling us that the actions of God on behalf of

Israel are a songwriter's fantasy. We can pretend that things like fire from heaven happened, but they really didn't.

This foreshadows the story of Israel's entry into the promised land as recorded in Joshua. The story begins with the unmistakable actions of God when the walls of Jericho fall down (6:20), but after this the battles continue with few signs of direct divine intervention. God is presented as involved in the ongoing battles for the control of Canaan, but not obviously so. After the Jericho story, no more walls come tumbling down.

In the Grand Narrative, the story of the children of Abraham begins and ends with a connection to a particular piece of land. The book of Joshua affirms this connection. This particular land was given to the people as a gift (1:11; 2:9, 24) for their use by God (chs. 13–22). This means that the land cannot belong to anyone else.

So God gave "us" this land as a gift. This God was with us (1:5), and his primary characteristic was strength and power (4:24). God's strength was directly tied to military strength (note the "commander of the armies of the Lord" in 5:14). The problem arose when God failed to deliver the land as promised. This was a particular problem for the returning exilic community, who shared the land with those who are already there, while operating under the control of the Persians (e.g. Ezra 9:9, Nehemiah 2:9, 10).

Within the story of Joshua, the actions of God become much less obvious. For example, in the second battle, God's actions are *against* Israel because of sin (7:1–12). But these actions, and God's subsequent actions *on behalf of* Israel (8:1–24), are only seen in the results of the battle. God gave specific commands to Joshua but did nothing miraculous. So the battles continued, largely without God's actions being obvious. If God was on their side, they won, otherwise they lost. Logically this led to the notion that, in general, we can tell whether God is on our side by whether we win battles. Thus, we can only see God's actions in retrospect, and even then exactly what God does is unclear.

This may lead to two different conclusions. The first is that we need not prepare for battle, since we will win if God is on our side. The second and opposite conclusion is that we must prepare and arm ourselves, then fight, and we will then win, which will prove that God is on our side and approves of our expanded militarism.[2]

In either case, the solution to difficult relationships with our neighbors is handled in the same way. No discussions are possible, no treaties

---

2. and guess which option gets chosen most often.

Old Testament—the bad news

allowed (Deuteronomy 7:1, 2). For the exilic community, this is a rather odd starting point, since they did not have the independence necessary to even field a military, never mind attack their neighbors. What it did mean is a strict separation from their neighbors, with no fraternizing allowed (Ezra 9:1, 2). This disconnection from neighboring peoples and the militarism it requires is reinforced repeatedly in many parts of the Grand Narrative.

This becomes even odder when we remember the situation in which the returning exiles find themselves. In describing their neighbors, they sometimes used the standard formula for the people of the land found in the Grand Narrative ("the Canaanites, the Hittites, the Perizzites, the Jebusites, the Ammonites, the Moabites, the Egyptians, and the Amorites;" Ezra 9:1). The book of Ezra acknowledges that some of them are worshipers of the same God, while denying that they are true Israelites (Ezra 4:2). Yet historically we know that those former groups have disappeared, and the people of the land were actually fellow children of Abraham, those who did not go into exile in Babylon.

The stories of Joshua incited/encouraged/reinforced an attitude toward their neighbors under the assumption that these people were utterly different from the returning exiles, even as they likely knew that their neighbors were actually estranged family. In this way, the denial of reality found in Exodus continued as it further alienated the returning exiles from their experience. And it continued even in the absence of God's direct intervention. God's will is only knowable after the fact (e.g. after they lose the battle), or in the voice of leaders. Leaders follow God fearlessly (1:7), and must be respected (4:14). The gift of the land is also constantly in danger of being revoked due to sin (7:12) or the people not following God's law (8:34–35). A key part of this law is separation and unwillingness to interact with others positively, even with potential allies.

In case we are tempted to think that this is a problem only for the ancient or modern Jewish community, it is also important to note how key these ideas were to many others in history. This is the basic attitude of many Christian armies and missionaries as they battled their way into Europe, Africa, the Americas, and most parts of the world. It still forms the basis for modern American ideals like manifest destiny and exceptionalism.

It is also important to step back and understand the notion of salvation that is found within this scenario. Salvation is for us. Salvation is God saving us (which turns out to be us saving ourselves) from them. "Them" includes everyone who is not us. This strict separation means that violence is our only option when confronted with conflict. In fact, inside the promised land, violence is our only option even when not confronted with conflict. After all, the nations who inhabited that land before Joshua arrived did nothing to threaten Israelite existence except refuse to simply disappear. Much the same could be said of indigenous people in North or South America.

Ideally this violent salvation is enacted by the God of power-and-might, but in his absence we are commanded to act similarly. So any relationship with the people around us is necessarily violent, and we are to be ashamed of those situations that are not (Joshua 9). Conquest is both goal and means and defines us as true people of the God of conquest.

And then . . .

The postexilic community had no opportunity to enact the policies they idealized in the book of Joshua. They were under Persian control, as were the groups around them. The Persians had no reason to desire intertribal genocide among its various groups. So even as the returned exiles adopted the Joshua stories to formulate their identity, they knew that this ideal could not be the end of the story. They lived in the promised land but were surrounded by people who were not "supposed to" be there. Neither the desires of God nor the actions of God nor their own actions were sufficient to create the world as they thought it should be.

This is easily contrasted with the endings of countless movies. At the end of many movies, the survivors are delivered to a place of love, peace, and safety, a place where they are firmly in control of their own fate. Imagine how different the ending of the movie would be if this place of safety was actually still under the control of the bad guys. This is the situation of the returning exiles. God had delivered them back to the land God had given them, a land "flowing with milk and honey," but both the milk and honey were distributed according to the dictates of their Persian overlords.

This disjunction is addressed in the book of Judges. In Judges, the people of Israel have entered the promised land and have adopted the correctly antagonistic relationship to the peoples around them. But the other peoples were still there. So despite the simple truth that God loved them more than anyone else (remembering this from Deuteronomy 7:6), not everything was as good as it could be (this is the general lesson from Judges 1:17–36). Part of the problem was the younger generation, who were not

Old Testament—the bad news

as good as the elders used to be (2:10).³ God had a larger purpose in this as well, putting temptations in their way to test them (2:3) and teach them how to be strong in battle (3:2). The wars that arose from this were also part of God's plan to punish those who did wrong (9:56, 57). The clear distinction between *us* and *them* in the above description of the problems that face *us* also means that ethnic purity was central to religious faithfulness (3:6).

All this relied on the local hero, who had the special gifts necessary to carry out the task of leadership (13:2–5). This person may not always have been the smartest person in the room (Samson and his father stand out here, Judges 13–16) and may have risen out of a rather humble beginning (Jephthah, son of a prostitute, Judges 11), but he gained glory and honor through war (8:22). Songs of victory were sung in honor of these heroes (ch. 5). The hero may die in old age as an honored member of society (8:32) or may die heroically in battle (16:30). The correct response of the people was to follow the leader without question (6:14, 34, 35).

While some verses point to occasional problems arising from the conflict between rich and poor (5:10–12), in general the system worked to ensure peace and security for all ("and the land had rest . . ." 3:30; 5:31, 8:28). As in Joshua, the whole system was guaranteed by God, who rescued the people when they repented (10:15–16).

One of the outcomes of telling the story in this way is to set out the ideal responsibilities of the ordinary people. In Judges, their task was obedience. This is usually set out as obedience to God (Judges 2:11) but consistently worked out as obedience to authority figures. Disobedience to the laws and commands of God led to repeated dire consequences ("the people did evil in the sight of the Lord, so . . ."). Peace could only be restored by the hero figure, who would bring about peace if the people followed him without question in his military conquests.

Shifting back to the postexilic community, the stories of Judges created an ideal of a very passive people. They were to follow the priests or the military leaders. In ordinary times, this meant continued financial support for the priesthood (a reality conspicuously absent in Judges). In bad times, it meant leaving the crops in the field and marshaling the resources necessary for a military campaign (because an army marches on its stomach) while also risking their lives because the hero has said that God said so.

In all of this, the God of power-and-might remained relevant only through the demands this God made on the people. He no longer gave

---

3. It makes one wonder how old this general perception is.

direct aid but worked through the hero figure. This figure may or may not get more direct help from God (Samson does, but Deborah doesn't) but otherwise was mostly noticeable when the people disobeyed.

Here again, however, we need to take a step back to see how this looks from the perspective of the ordinary Israelite. In Jerusalem, there was a group of people (priests) who dictated the various rules for the people. Mostly these rules involved ordinary people bringing food to the priests, who offered it to God but also consumed it themselves (Nehemiah 10:32–39). These priests claimed that the peace and security of the land was built upon the continuation of this system.

This system did not always work as advertised. Regularly the peace and security of the land broke down, either because of internal or external pressures. When this happened, blame was placed not on the priests but on the ordinary people ("the Israelites did evil," a phrase repeated seven times in Judges). The text never bothers explaining what they did or why the various actions of the priesthood failed to make things right between the people and God. They did evil, they (not the leaders) got punished, and they (not the leaders) must fix it by blindly following the hero whom God had appointed.

The book of Judges accomplished this by simply writing the priesthood out of the story. In the absence of a central worship site, the text has no way to talk about how God was worshiped during the period of the Judges. But surely the priesthood appointed by Moses earlier in the story must have been doing something.

Jumping back again to the postexilic community, the absence of priests in the Judges story leads to a sense that the sin of the people (rather than the sins of the leaders) was the most likely cause of the current problems (here defined as Persian control over the promised land). As we have already noted, Persian control may not have been an actual problem for most of the people. They may also have gotten along just fine with their new neighbors. In fact, they appear to be getting along well enough to be intermarrying (Ezra 9:2).[4]

So the "problem" for which the priesthood was the only available solution (in the absence of God or appointed heroes) was one created by the priests themselves. They wrote this problem into the story of "who we are," creating a people willing to blame themselves for problems created by their leaders.

4. This arises out of the ancient theological quandary: What do you do when the heathen girl next door is really hot?

In this way, the writers of the Grand Narrative continued to provide ways of dealing with their situation that were not real options for their people. Whether the solution was direct intervention by God (Exodus), generalized genocide (Joshua), or the emergence of heroes to rescue them from their oppressors (Judges), the stories ignored the real situation and realistic options. They did reinforce passivity and obedience, as well as the perspective that suggested that the leaders were in the best position to define possible problems and solutions.

Kings

Having chosen the God of power-and-might as described in the Exodus story, the writers of the Grand Narrative needed to continue the story while providing some explanation for the absence of those sorts of actions of God in their present. They also needed to explain how they got to Babylon in the first place. This was especially important in the community during and after the exile. The failure of the power-and-might God to intervene before, during, or after the exile was not something that could simply be ignored. More obviously, the exile itself could not be ignored. Whether or not they chose to think of the return from Babylon as a salvation experience, they needed to respond to the exile and the lack of plagues, manna, and military intervention from the sky.

As we have seen, the Grand Narrative provided excuses for God's absence. It was the people's sin (Judges 2:11–14 and regularly as part of the paradigm in Judges) that caused God's judgment and the removal of salvation.

So salvation comes through obedience to the covenant. Besides this, the Grand Narrative includes another major way for the people to be saved. The king's task was to save the people (1 Samuel 10:1). That's what a king was for. So God chose the king, whose task it was to save the people, and the priests in the Temple used animal sacrifice to propitiate God, so that the sins of the people did not give God a reason not to fulfill his part of the covenant. Thus salvation should have come both from God and from the King. The sins of the people should have no longer been an issue. The system has ways of dealing with sin that should have been sufficient to bring salvation and prosperity to Israel. Yet clearly both systems failed in some manner, and the people of Israel were led away into exile in Babylon.

You Are Not Going to Heaven (and why it doesn't matter)

At first it might seem that a discussion of kingship does not belong in the "bad news" section of this book. After all, if we are looking for an understanding of salvation that is grounded in lived experience, the kingship is certainly a major part of the lived experience of the people of Israel. A more careful study of the way the Grand Narrative portrays kingship, however, shows that its view of kingship is so idealized as to provide little basis for a way forward in the concrete realities of history and politics.

The Grand Narrative generally blames the kings for the downfall of the kingdom of Israel. 2 Kings 21:11 is a key passage here, where the destruction of Jerusalem is foretold by the prophets because of the sins of King Manasseh. Since the king had replaced God as the savior of the people, at least in the way the story is told in Kings, the sins of the king were now responsible for the decision by God to call the Babylonians to conquer Israel. Note that the Grand Narrative never blames the priesthood (although some of the prophets do). Apparently the sacrifices in the Temple could not atone for the sins of the king. He was judged on a simple up-or-down basis (see the many repetitions of "the king did evil" or "the king did what was right" in 2 Kings).

Whatever reasons or explanations the Grand Narrative provides for the failure of kingship to bring salvation, there was little doubt of the failure. The king's task was to save the people, and the people of Israel were defeated by the Babylonians. While some parts of the Old Testament still hold out hope for monarchy as a system (e.g. Isaiah 32:1), it was a system that was wholly dependent on the character of the king.

For the postexilic community, the kingship paradigm entered the realm of fantasy and left behind the day-to-day realities of lived experience. The Persians did not allow the Israelites to appoint a king, so the whole issue of kingship could be safely raised without disturbing the status quo among the leadership.

Temple

As the Grand Narrative of the people of Israel, these books functioned both as retrospect and prospect. That is, they answered the question "How did we get here?" as well as the question "Who are we and how do we live now?" What is so interesting is that, in the Persian world, while the Israelite monarchy had been abolished by the Persian rulers, the temple institutions were intact and maintained some sort of significant status. Yet it must be recognized that the temple system appears to be unable to deliver the promised salvation, since any notion of salvation would have included independence from foreign rule.

This is an important silence in the Grand Narrative. The salvation (survival and ongoing well-being) of the people of Israel is ensured by the ongoing sacrificial system as controlled and maintained by the priests in Jerusalem. Yet in every stage of Israelite history (as recorded in the Grand Narrative), the priests are unable to provide this salvation. Despite this, the Grand Narrative never blames or even mentions the failure of the priesthood. So even in the Persian period, the priesthood retains significant (and increasing) power over the people despite their ongoing failure to save the people from Persian domination.

The temple system worked differently from the monarchy. While the task of the king was to bring the salvation offered by God, the temple had no direct role in bringing salvation. Rather, the temple functioned in a number of ways to ensure that God had no excuse not to uphold God's part of the covenant. Whether God was thought to work directly or through the king, if the temple was functioning as it should, salvation should have happened.

On the other hand, the Persian period appears to be one of relative stability and peace for Israel. It is only with the coming of the Seleucids (190 BC) that the question of efficacy would likely have become pressing. Both the Persian rulers and the Ptolomaic Greek rulers mostly adopted a live-and-let-live attitude toward the Jewish people. With the coming of the Seuleucid Greeks, the persecution of the Jewish people led to a more pressing need for salvation.

It is impossible to know whether the Israelites during the Persian period thought they needed to be saved from the Persians. Perhaps they preferred the benign neglect of the Persians to the ambitions and instability of the earlier monarchy.

Still, as Persian rule dragged on for decades (roughly 520 -330 BC), the temple's ability to ensure salvation must have been called into question. Exactly how righteous did Israel have to be to be worthy of God's rescue? If righteousness was the issue, was it the people's righteousness or the leader's? And if righteousness was really the issue, then was the temple institution really necessary? If temple practices failed to bring God's action, then what were they for? Did it make sense to continue to pay the priesthood 10 percent of your produce every year when they were consistently unable to live up to their end of the deal? Or was the threat that things could always get worse?

This scenario suggests that the purpose of the temple institution was to maintain the authority and the income of the priesthood. That is, the purpose of the priesthood was to maintain itself. In the book of Nehemiah, this is stated rather baldly ("On that day men were appointed over the chambers for the stores, the contributions, the first fruits, and the tithes, to gather into them the portions required by the law for the priests and for the Levites from the fields belonging to the towns; for Judah rejoiced over the priests and the Levites who ministered." 12:44). In fact, it almost seems like the purpose of the people was to maintain the priesthood.

This oddity is likely familiar to many people who are part of a church. Does the church exist to serve the people, or does the church exist to keep the pastor employed? After all, when the pastor speaks about the need to continue the ministries of the church, this includes his salary. The system becomes a self-perpetuating loop. The church is necessary because it says it is. We grant it the authority it has, based on a book we follow because the church says we should.

The Grand Narrative provided the ideological basis for this system and established the authority of the priesthood in four ways. First, the priesthood was instituted at Sinai with the selection of Aaron (Exodus 28:1). This provided the priesthood with a connection to the Exodus paradigm, to covenant and law. Thus, the priesthood was presented as simply integral to the system. The connection between God and the people was portrayed as being unimaginable without the priesthood. It is also likely that a world without animal sacrifice was generally unimaginable, since the consumption of meat requires killing, and the ritual of killing would have automatically included recognition of the taking of a life (unlike our modern world where we slaughter animals by the millions with no thought for the life that was). The alternative to centralized priesthood—sacrifice outside the control of the Jerusalem priesthood—was strongly condemned in law and narrative (Deuteronomy 12:2–7, 2 Kings 12:3). So control of the means of sacrifice (clearly established by contrast to the "high places") meant that the priesthood was necessary to ensure the covenant.

Second, the priests' connection to salvation also meant that the priesthood was necessary to maintain the status quo. The Persian period appears to be one of relative peace and security for the people of Judea. Yes, there may have been some hope for a return of the Israelite kingship, but the Grand Narrative does not portray that option as being necessarily better. In Kings, the welfare of the people becomes dependent upon the actions of the king. No matter how righteous the people, apparently a bad king may cause all kinds of calamity to fall on Israel. There is no way for the people to atone for the sins of the king, and no legitimate means to depose a king, so a king is a risky way to do leadership. Priests, on the other hand, are generally presented as people who pose no threat to the people, so changing the priesthood would presumably have no effect on the political scene. In this way, the priesthood took significant authority over the people without being culpable for bad things that befell them.

Third, the priest's connection to sacrifice meant that they were a natural part of the regular rhythms of life. In a world of subsistence agriculture, festivals marked important events, but also provided something to look forward to in the dreary weeks and months of repetitious toil. All festivals were linked to the temple (in the Grand Narrative, if not in actual practice), which created a psychological connection between priests and celebration. This linked the priesthood not only to salvation but also thanksgiving for harvest and the celebration of special events such as childbirth. In this way, a world without priests became simply unimaginable.

Finally, priests were presented as being necessary for the future. Sacrifice and temple ritual were the means to God's favor, so priests would have been a necessary part of any reform or rebellion or vision of new Israel. So the prophets presented the New Israel with a rebuilt Jerusalem and refurbished temple, rather than a new Israel with its capital at Shechem or Lacish or any number of other, more logical places to put a capital. Yet whatever the future hope, if Yahweh was the only one who can affect this future, then any plan for this future must include the priests.

In these ways, the Grand Narrative (and significant other parts of the Old Testament) provides a vision of salvation that necessarily included the priesthood. Whether or not this was or is true, it failed to recognize the failure of the priesthood to bring about salvation in the life of the people of Israel. During the times of the kings, the priests were unable to affect the future of the people, since it all rested in the goodness of the king himself. Later, during the exile, the priests became unemployed (due to lack of a temple), yet God brought the people back anyway. Then after the rebuilding of the temple after the exile, the priests were unable to ensure God's favor, insofar as they were unable to bring about the end of foreign occupation. Yet the Old Testament refuses to acknowledge this reality. Somehow after hundreds of years of failure, the priesthood remains key to Israel's salvation.

You Are Not Going to Heaven (and why it doesn't matter)

Prophets

In many ways, the prophets are the trickiest group to try to deal with as we try to connect the Old Testament with our current situation (whatever that may be). Their writings continue to be crucial for many who work for the health and well-being of the world, so I do not want to suggest that they are of no value. But it is also important to recognize the inherent problem they pose to us.

The writings of the prophets (generally Isaiah and onward in the Old Testament) were responses to the various crises of the Israelite people. Mostly these were the death and destruction that occurred as various empires conquered Israel. The prophets proclaimed these as the will of God (the God who fights *against* us) due to the failure of Israel to live up to its side of the covenant it had made with God. These included the sins of the people, the leadership, the priests, the wealthy, the kings, and even the other prophets.

This is a tricky idea to bring forward to our time. However we choose to understand the situation of the prophets, in our time the church has too often seen itself as the weapon that God is using to punish "evildoers." This idea can be traced historically through the Crusades, the conquest of "the New World," and the church's approach to the education of children. But we do not need to go back into history to illustrate this point. This kind of rhetoric was also used by some churches to explain the American invasions of Afghanistan and Iraq. So whether this is through war on an international scale or simply locally ostracizing people who don't fit, this sort of rhetoric has led the church into doing more evil than it has prevented.

Prophetic rhetoric also allows the victors to proclaim, "This war was God's will," and those sitting comfortably in safety to say, "That disaster was God's will." Too often this is used as an excuse not to respond with love and kindness. It also allows us to feel morally superior to victims of natural or human-made disaster. This is not helpful. However we are going to define salvation, it should not include kicking people when they are down. The good news we proclaim is either good news for everyone or it is good news for no one.

Another difficulty in using the prophetic paradigm is that the connections they make between cause and effect assumes the God of power-and-might. The logic is simple and tempting. God is really big and ultimately just. If bad stuff happens, and God does not intervene, it must mean that

God specifically desired this to happen. Therefore, someone must have been bad. The only question is who was bad and what we should do about them.

There is certainly much to be learned from examining the causes of human-made disasters and not repeating these mistakes. It does not help to bring God into the discussion simply because there is no logical connection between perceived cause and effect. It is even less helpful to bring God into the discussion because we don't want to be honest about our own culpability. Did the people in the war die because their leaders were evil and God is punishing them, or did they die because we shot them (or our taxes paid for the weapons that killed them)?

While the prophets do encourage us to think about cause and effect and also encourage us to think about the larger will of God for the world, they are too easily used to avoid serious thinking. In the Persian period, they allowed the survivors to blame "them" for the mess they were in, or to blame the victims. They also led the people to see military power as the major way that change could happen, leaving control in the hands of their self-appointed leaders. Salvation, then, lay in the hands of God and his divinely ordained representatives. The task of the people was to be good and obedient.

Messiah

As the Persian period dragged on, the failure of king, priest, and the God of power-and-might to bring salvation (in the form of political independence) must have become obvious. The disjunction between expectation and reality likely caused a variety of reactions, from denial to loss of faith to loss of hope. For many, on the other hand, there may have been little reason to desire political independence. For subsistence farmers, the goal of life is survival. If the Persian period provided the political stability necessary for basic survival, the average Israelite may have had few complaints.

If we continue to ground our notion of salvation in the political and economic conditions of regular people, it is possible to see the Persian period as one of peace and stability. While the Persians were ultimately in control of affairs in Judea, Persia was a long way from Jerusalem. The leaders of the local Israelite population who would have been encountered by the ordinary people would have been Israelites like themselves. So long as the taxes extracted by the central government were not so large as to significantly threaten survival, there may have been little reason to believe that political independence would have improved conditions.

You Are Not Going to Heaven (and why it doesn't matter)

For the average Israelite peasant (roughly 90 percent of the population), the encounter with "government" would have been via the forced extraction of their resources. Officials, likely accompanied by soldiers, would regularly appear and take some of the harvest (including animals, crops and even children—see 1 Samuel 8:11–17). Exactly who these people were and where the harvest was going may have mattered little. Jewish authorities came to take some of the harvest. Whether these precious resources went to Jerusalem or Persia was of little consequence. The important question was how much they took, rather than where it was going. It may be that the authorities in Jerusalem were able to persuade the people that taking this harvest to maintain the temple in Jerusalem was in their own best interest, but we can't really know how successful this program was (or whether the Jerusalem authorities even cared what the peasants thought).

Within this reality, it was the leaders in Jerusalem who were most likely to be interested in political independence. They were the ones who felt in need of "salvation." The average people of Israel were just as likely to think about salvation *from* the rulers in Jerusalem as salvation *for* the rulers in Jerusalem. For the rulers themselves, salvation from Persian rule would have meant greater independence. It also would have meant that more of the resources extracted from the people could be retained in Jerusalem rather than passed on to Persia.

On the other hand, the Persians were certainly an overwhelming force and unlikely to go away in the near future. For some in Jerusalem, then, expectation shifted to the great Someday. (Someday God will . . .) This hope for divine rescue was built into the Grand Narrative as well as the Prophets and Writings. The question of how salvation might come was also built into their central texts. This future hope could be based on the Exodus, monarchic or priestly paradigms. It certainly included no action by the peasants except in obedience to their rulers. After all, their salvation was not at issue.

The future hope we find built into the Grand Narrative and the prophets is largely of the Messianic type. It requires a central (human) king-figure, who will destroy Israel's enemies and bring about the reign of God (that, not surprisingly, would have included major roles for the current leadership in Jerusalem). In many ways, Messianic hope is a combination of the exodus/king/priest fantasies noted above. Messianic hope is focused on the historical future and ideally within the near future. The Messiah may be alive today, waiting for . . . (and here is where conditions arose). These conditions, then, are also likely to be historical and may be linked to

Old Testament—the bad news

some notion of salvation. The Messiah will come and do X, but only after Y happens. Both X and Y are open to a variety of narratives, depending on the perspective and interests of the speaker.

In some ways, this is similar to the Superman myth. Superman will come and rescue us, but only certain people are worthy of this (= white Americans?). But does Superman come and save us because we are inherently worthy, or only when we act in a way that is worthy? So when Superman fails to show up, is it because we are unworthy? What is it that makes us better than those we are being rescued from?

It is also important to remember that for many others in the Jewish community, life just went on. Survival was the goal, agriculture was the means to that goal, and God's place in the rhythm of work/eat/sleep was so obvious that it required little thought. The temple authorities and the secular authorities (who may have been the same people) came to take their part of the harvest (as they defined it), and the peasants gathered on the Sabbath and went to the temple for major festivals because that is what a Jew did (or for any of a myriad of other social/cultural/personal/religious reasons). In this world, salvation was a discussion that happened among people with the resources to provide the time for education and leisure. We have no way of knowing what ordinary people thought, what sort of access they had to the "official" teachings of their own scribes, or how much they believed about any of it (just as we today often have little knowledge of what people inside or outside the church actually believe about what they are told).

Messianic hope became a major force when the need became more pressing. In roughly 200 BC, the Seleucids overran the Ptolomies, who had been ruling the territory of Israel. While both groups were part of a larger Hellenistic movement, the Ptolomies were much less aggressive in enforcing Hellenistic practices than were the Seleucids (especially in regard to the worship of Greek gods). With the widespread persecution of Jews by the Seleucids, the "someday" of Messianic hope became a "someday really soon." It is also clear from history that many Jews did not see this as a passive waiting for someone else to rescue them. The various rebellions during the two centuries before and after Jesus show us that many Jews viewed salvation as both historical and participatory. The question was one of how and when.

Conclusion

The official documents we have from the second temple period tell of a world where the people of Israel lived in an ongoing covenantal relationship with their God. The maintenance of this covenant had certain real-world implications for the people, both in threat and reward. Despite this very clear focus on this-world realities, there was also the temptation to wait for salvation to come from outside normal experience. Despite their ongoing experience of very human systems that operated without world-altering intervention from God, some chose to wait for this type of intervention.

This Grand Narrative notwithstanding, it would seem apparent that these hopes were not being fulfilled. God no longer sent Moses figures to inflict plagues on Israel's enemies. The perfect king was not forthcoming, and the people continued to deal with the very human leaders in Jerusalem and Persia. Sacrifice in the temple was not being particularly effective in fixing the relationship between Israel and its God and thus bringing about God's rescue. All these were often wrapped together in a Messiah fantasy that continued to exist only in dreams.

Whatever their theology of salvation, reality suggests that there was still something not happening, at least on the big rescue front. The destruction of the Temple in 70 AD came and went, and no salvation was offered. At least, no salvation was offered of the exodus/king/priest/Messiah type. So either we need to abandon a biblical notion of salvation, or we need to find other parts of the Bible that offer other solutions.

For Christians, the answers are usually found in the New Testament. This, I am going to suggest, is only partly true. There are significant parts of the Old Testament that I have ignored and that do provide a way forward (see chapter 4). And the New Testament is also guilty of trying to ground salvation outside human experience. It is to this reality that we now turn.

3

New Testament—the bad news

I REALIZE THAT THIS chapter will come as a surprise to many readers. If you've grown up in church, you're probably expecting to read that the Old Testament has the bad news but the New Testament contains only good news.[1] While this analysis is generally false, it is especially not true for the question I am addressing here. While the Old Testament is guilty of avoiding reality when it comes to the question of salvation, the New Testament is even more so because it often refuses to deal with the reality of the central character it proclaims.

Jesus died on a cross. He was tortured to death as a political-religious troublemaker. The early church was forced to deal with the cross. It was inescapable. People who heard about the Jesus movement were bound to find out that he was tortured to death by Roman authorities. There was no miraculous escape, no divine intervention, just a dead guy on a cross. So the church needed to deal with this event up front, rather than trying to pretend it didn't happen.

The cross is hardly a normal ending to a savior story. In almost every hero movie you've ever seen, the good guy miraculously escapes at the last possible moment. Then he (or occasionally she) roars back in triumph, slaughtering the bad guys (and gals?) on all sides, rescuing the ones who need to be saved, and making everything good again. Yes, you might be able to think of a few exceptions, but they are few and they are exceptions.

---

1. On the other hand, if you haven't grown up in church, you might not be at all surprised, because for you the New Testament is definitely full of bad news (see Matthew 10:14–15; 13:41–42, etc.).

You Are Not Going to Heaven (and why it doesn't matter)

This was also the kind of Messiah many Jewish people were expecting (assuming they were expecting a Messiah at all). The Messiah was to be a prophet/priest/king hero figure who would drive out the Roman armies and established God's kingdom on earth. There were variations on this theme, but the basic plot line was assumed. No Messianic expectation ended with the Romans still firmly in control. Defeating the Romans was what it meant to be a Messiah. "Dead on a cross" was not part of the job description.

This type of expectation was the logical result of the Old Testament story. As we saw in the last chapter, the writers of the Old Testament chose to write a certain kind of story about their relationship with God. It focused on actions of God of the Exodus type. This led naturally to future expectations of someone who would come and do the whole Moses thing again, who would deliver them miraculously from their enemies.

So the early church needed to deal with the reality of a crucified Messiah. Now I realize that the Gospels do not end at the cross. There are the resurrection and ascension to take into account as well. But as an ending to a Messiah story, even the resurrection is finally unsatisfying. Yes, Jesus rose again, but quietly. There were no blaring trumpets, blazing lights, or angelic hosts. Even the birth of Jesus had more pizzazz than the resurrection. It is like watching the ending of your favorite hero movie with the sound off, and without the special effects.

Jesus rose from the grave without any witnesses. The Gospels do not record the event, so we aren't even helped to imagine what it looked or sounded like. Later he was seen by his followers, but close friends are not the most credible witnesses. He didn't show up at the temple to say, "I told you so." He didn't walk up to Pilate and decapitate him with a mighty stroke of a heavenly sword.

So even in his resurrection, he didn't do the hero thing properly. According to the standard hero narrative, there needs to be vindication. There need to be public demonstrations of power and wrath. At the very least, there needs to be some sort of movement that gets rid of the Romans and installs a godly ruler in their place. Yes, we can make all this spiritual, but we do this because we need it. We spiritualize to avoid disappointment.

Instead of these things, what did Jesus do? Each Gospel tells the story in a slightly different way. Mark ends with no actual appearances by Jesus recorded.[2] A man in a white robe told the women to tell the disciples to go to Galilee, where they will see him (16:7), but Mark does not include any

2. Mark 16:9–20 are not part of the original Gospel.

stories where this actually happened. Always the mysterious Gospel, Mark ends with the promise of Jesus' appearance, but the story simply ends there.

John ends with Jesus speaking to Peter and John (21:15–22), then a brief note that he's run out of paper (21:25). The ending of John and the stories of Jesus after the resurrection are further complicated by John's double ending. John appears to conclude in 20:30, 31, then awkwardly adds another chapter. However you want to understand this, there are no stories about major public events that demonstrate to the world that Jesus was risen. And there is nothing to indicate what happened to Jesus. So both Mark and John end rather abruptly, with a sense that the story of Jesus remains unfinished.

Matthew's conclusion is the most dramatic. It ends on a mountain in Galilee, with a final teaching from Jesus. It contains a definite call for the movement to continue and what almost looks like a promise to stay ("I am with you," 28:20). And there it just ends. Jesus promised to be with us always, yet he's gone (at least physically). Again, spiritualizing arises out of necessity. In what sense is Jesus with us, when he is so clearly absent? The "spiritual" explanation is the only reasonable one. So after carefully recording the birth, life, death, and resurrection of Jesus, Matthew doesn't bother to tell us where Jesus went or how.

Thus, three of the Gospels end without resolving the question of where Jesus went after the resurrection. Luke, on the other hand, records two different accounts of Jesus' ascension (24:51 and Acts 1:9), but they say little more than that Jesus has gone into heaven.[3] Acts adds a promise of return (1:11), but this is quietly given to a small group of followers rather than as a booming voice from heaven that proclaims the truth of Jesus' message to the whole world.

So even in his return from the grave, Jesus was a very unsatisfying messianic hero. In this light, it is not really surprising that most Jews rejected him. The resurrection and ascension did not resolve the problem created by the cross. If the savior of humankind was killed by the bad guys, where was the great victory? How can we avoid the logical conclusion that Jesus was a failed Messiah?

In all this, we need to remember that salvation was supposed to have real-world consequences. If Jesus' life, death, and resurrection were somehow supposed to heal the break between us and God, what were the signs that this had happened? The expectations, while varied, were clear. The sign

---

3. The Greek word *ouranos* means both "heaven" and "sky."

of the coming of the Messiah, the sign of salvation, was to be the establishment of the kingdom of God on earth, with the Messiah (or at least someone from the line of David) on a physical throne in Jerusalem. The precedent arose logically out of the Old Testament, with the examples of David, Joshua, and Moses. It arose also on the basis of a view of salvation based on the Exodus story. If Moses was the paradigm, and if the Romans were the new Egyptians, then Jesus simply did not succeed. But even more basically, the expectation arose logically out of nearly any notion of what it means to be a savior of the people.

In response to these factors, the early church took on the challenge of attempting to proclaim Jesus as Messiah in the face of the reality of the cross. They also spread the news that Jesus brought a new relationship with God, that he was a *means* of salvation. They further took on the challenge of proclaiming this salvation in some sort of real-world framework. Ultimately, however, what they often failed to do in this attempt was to make sense of salvation in the light of Jesus of Nazareth. While there are parts of the New Testament that take Jesus seriously, much of the New Testament resorts to easy fall-back positions. These positions also result in the church no longer being responsible to continue the mission and message of Jesus. The message of Jesus is lost in a message about Jesus.

OPTION A—APOCALYPTICISM

Just as the Jewish community after the exile preferred the power-and-might God of the Exodus to the real God of the Persian community, the disciples of Jesus preferred the power-and-might Messiah of legend to the real Jesus of Nazareth, the crucified one. So they resorted to the great Someday. Against all the evidence that they had just seen in the form of the suffering servant, God was returned to his form as the Great Powerful Rescuer in the Sky, and Jesus of Nazareth was stripped of his humble robes to don the armor of the rescuing hero.

This is vitally important to our understanding of both the New Testament and Jesus. The New Testament proclaims that Jesus of Nazareth was the Savior sent from God. This savior lived, taught, healed and died, without any obvious repetition of the exodus story. So one possible conclusion is that God, as made flesh in Jesus, does not work in the big, flashy way that the exodus story proclaims. Instead, God works in small ways, in the movement of seemingly insignificant people, in the healing of the suffering and pain of the world. This is certainly one logical conclusion from the proclamation that Jesus' life was the ideal representation of God.

Instead, many parts of the New Testament revert to the God of the exodus and try to fit Jesus into the mold. The simplest way to do this was to write the story so that the historical Jesus becomes Act One in a two-act savior drama. Act One was the suffering servant, with the cross taking central place. Act Two will be Jesus returning to do the job the "right way," like Moses and David and the other great heroes of old. So the teachings and example of Jesus get buried beneath the fantasy Jesus, with the drama now expanded to include all of earth and heaven.

Gospels

The earthly Jesus does not entirely disappear from the Gospels, and the movement to rewrite the mission and message of Jesus did not always go smoothly. Mark, likely the oldest Gospel, seems to recognize how poorly the apocalyptic Jesus fit with the rest of the story. He crammed all the apocalyptic traditions into a single section, chapter 13. The rest of his story has a very earthly Jesus with a mission and message focused on the coming kingdom of God. But this kingdom is not linked to slaughtered Romans or imperial pretensions. Neither is it linked to a spiritual plane severed from the social and political reality of everyday Galilee. Mark's enigmatic and mysterious Gospel gives us few simple answers for the questions that plague our world, but the mission to do something is clear, to follow in the Way without guarantees of success. In fact, the only sure thing seems to be opposition.

It is this Jesus that fits so poorly with the usual apocalyptic traditions, where the suffering is all on the other side. Apocalyptic traditions usually work out of the usual savior myth, with the savior bringing retribution upon "our" enemies (who of course are also God's enemies) as "just" recompense for what they did to us. So God appears as savior in our revenge fantasy, acting much like the enemies whom we characterize as evil. Somehow this is okay, because God is beyond human judgment, but it does show that our fantasy of power and destruction is remarkably similar to that of the "bad guys."

Yet Mark's apocalyptic section does not indulge these fantasies. Instead, he continues to focus on the suffering of the believing community (13:9, 11, 13–19), rather than the suffering of our enemies. Mark says nothing about the events that follow the return of Jesus but speaks about the events that precede it. So Mark does not allow us to escape into some sort of victory fantasy. He continues to ground his gospel in the work of the community in a world that opposes it, a world that fails to see the greater vision of the coming kingdom and that fails to follow.

The gospel of John, too, portrays a Jesus who is not focused on a final apocalyptic victory. Whatever we make of John's Gospel, it does not point toward a time of cosmic triumph in an earthly battle between good and evil. John 21:22, 23 does mention Jesus speaking of his return but without any mention of what this might look like.

Matthew and Luke repeat and refine much of Mark 13 (Matthew 25, Luke 21), and also share other apocalyptic judgment traditions. Both Gospels move into apocalyptic mode much sooner than did Mark. John the baptizer sets up the apocalyptic Jesus by issuing a warning to the Pharisees and Sadducees that those who do not bear fruit will be "cut down and thrown into the fire" (Matthew 3:7–10//Luke 3:7–9, and repeated by Jesus in Matthew 7:19). They both continue with numerous passages about the coming of the Son of Man, both its sudden appearance and its spectacular nature (see Matthew 12:39–59, 17:23–35).

This way of presenting the story of Jesus suggests that Matthew and Luke did not really believe that the way of Jesus is itself salvation. Rather, the message of Jesus is a message of future salvation, a message about salvation deferred. The real consequences of salvation are shifted to a longed-for future, when the Son of Man will come and do the work that Jesus failed to do. Even though Matthew claims that the death of Jesus brings forgiveness of sin (26:28, a claim Luke doesn't make), the real actions of God in bringing salvation are for some future time. Their basic paradigm for how God acts in the world are rooted in the picture found in the Old Testament passages we looked at in chapter 2. In this picture, Jesus can announce salvation but fails to bring it about, and his life does not provide a true picture of how God really acts in the world. Or at least the current actions of God are only a stop-gap measure, while God waits to reveal God's true character in the future.

This emphasis on the final judgment significantly changes our perception of who Jesus was and what it means to follow. It means that Jesus' life only revealed to us the "for now" way of God (the way of suffering love), while his apocalyptic words revealed the final way of God, the way of violent overthrow of enemies through superior force. This becomes the "true" meaning of salvation, as we become one with God through God's violent overthrow of our current political and economic systems. But mostly it means that the God we have been experiencing throughout most of human history is not the real God. If the real God is the one revealed in the violent overthrow of human systems, to be replaced by systems of divine origin, then the real God remains conspicuously absent in human history. Certainly many have come proclaiming that their reform or revolution is that of God, but these always turn out to be amazingly human systems, ruled by the same laws of cause and effect as the ones that preceded them.

The apocalyptic God does not play by these rules. The apocalyptic God suspends cause and effect and creates a system though divine fiat. Natural cycles of weather, economics, and other natural and sociological systems are interrupted by major infusions of power from the "spiritual" realm. These interventions are obvious and dramatic, and are quite unlike the way God is usually experienced (assuming that God is experienced at all).

For the modern reader, it leads to a faith that focuses on individual actions without worrying about social consequences. Jesus becomes the one who provides and later enforces the rules, enforced by a reward/punishment system at the end. The world around me may be slowly falling apart, but I can follow the rules and expect to get rewarded.

In this scheme, the way of the suffering servant is just one of the rules, done for the sake of selfish gain. I do this for the reward, which will come later. The reward is then otherworldly, as the Son of Man ushers in a new age that is completely divorced from the current one. Old systems will fall, and the Son of Man will be seated on his throne. Democracy, consensus, and the judgment of the community will all be swept away, replaced by absolute monarchy. This means that there is no final value in working toward communities of justice and fairness; only individual rule-following matters.

In this way, the goal of salvation is shifted to the final judgment scene. We focus on the sheep and the goats (Matthew 25) and check to make sure we're one of the sheep. In this system, Jesus becomes Santa Claus, and we become the little children who are good so that Santa will bring us presents. There is no real salvation. Jesus is Santa, we are the kids, and all we can hope for is Santa's approval. We do not labor with Santa toward any goal. Santa does not abide with us, neither does Santa have any sort of larger plan for this world, so we don't have to worry about being part of it.

The Gospels, then, provide a variety of apocalyptic approaches to Jesus. Each of these is a response to the disjunction between the expectation of a power-and-might Messiah and the reality of a crucified Jesus. This disjunction will continue to follow us throughout this study. It cannot be ignored because it is key to our answer to the question of what salvation means.

Paul

Paul provides an additional example of a New Testament author who is focused on the return of Jesus to finish the task that he apparently failed to do originally. While Paul was generally focused on the cross and resurrection, he also expected certain things of the Messiah that Jesus failed to do, so his expectation shifted to the future. This affects his understanding of salvation, which is always grounded in a future apocalyptic hope.

Paul may be excused for his apocalyptic fixation because he knew little of the historical Jesus and was likely regularly involved in disagreements with those who did (such as Peter and Jesus' brother James, see Acts 15, 21 and Galatians 2). But this does mean that his views on salvation were based more on the Messiah he wants rather than the Jesus he had. Paul wanted the savior to come in good old-fashioned Exodus style. He wanted wrath for his (and presumably God's) enemies (1 Thessalonian 1:10, Romans 2:5). He wanted the Messiah who appears from heaven to pronounce judgment on evildoers (1 Corinthians 4:5; 10:11), while handing out rewards for those of us who have been good (Romans 2:7). Paul quickly left behind the earthly Jesus, and substituted the Messiah of apocalyptic fantasy.

Whatever we make of Paul's message (and there is much to be said in defense of Paul), we need to recognize that we have an advantage over Paul. We know for certain that Jesus did not return in Paul's lifetime as he expected. We are almost 2,000 years after the writings of Paul, and Jesus has not yet returned. Perhaps there is a lesson here. While Paul built his churches on the basis of an apocalyptic hope (Philippians 3:20), we can only do that by avoiding reality. This remains an option, but not one to build God's kingdom on. Trying to envision a future based on the-God-who-failed-to-show-up is not promising. This is not to suggest that Paul is useless to us as we move forward. But it is to recognize that Paul is not always helpful. The glass that Paul looked through (1 Corinthians 13:12) was more opaque than he realized.

Revelation

The book of Revelation, of course, remains the primary text for apocalyptic Christianity. Much of what has already been said about apocalyptic salvation can also be applied to Revelation. The quiet ministry of the Galilean becomes a death-dealing, flame-throwing, world-destroying bloodbath where the blood of the lamb is overwhelmed by the blood of God's slain enemies. The church maintained its precarious position at the margins of the Roman social world by reveling in revenge fantasies (Revelation 6:10).

Revelation also added the element of purity to the story. The world is dirty, and we need to stay clean. Someday the Lamb will come to rescue his pure church, but until then the church must somehow manage to remain clean while living in a dirty world (3:4–5). This creates a significant distance between the church and the world around it, a distance that is abstract but that affects the way the church relates to its society.

If we look out at the world through these eyes, we see Satan at work. All individuals, institutions, and organizations belong to Satan, except for the church. Salvation, then, is the work of bringing someone out of that world into the community of purity (7:14). It is a work of cleansing, where the blood of the Lamb washes off the filth of the world and allows us to enter the church as clean individuals. This new-found cleanliness must be strictly maintained, for our new white garments are in constant danger of being soiled by contact with the dirt around us.

In this view, the work of God is taking place in the church, and only there. Salvation is a radical shift, and we have no expectation that Satan's institutions can be included in this work. The only solution to the problem is blood—both the blood of the lamb (12:11) and the blood of God's enemies (14:20).

What is important to note here is the radical shift this is from the view of salvation in Mark. Yes, Mark also includes an apocalyptic section in his gospel, but Mark has no interest in purity. In Mark, purity is the realm of the Pharisees. They constantly wash to keep clean (7:1–13), while Jesus eats with sinners (2:15–17).

Note that both Mark and Revelation agree that purity is a real issue. The new community of Jesus is called to live exemplary lives. The question is one of contagion. In Revelation, the mental image is of the church walking through a dirty world in white robes. Obviously contact with this world makes our robes dirty, and so is to be avoided. Anyone with small children lives by a similar code. If you dress children in their best clothing, you hope and strive to maintain that cleanliness. You don't encourage them to play in the dirt. You also don't allow them to play with friends who are sick because disease is often contagious.

Jesus in Mark insists that in the social/spiritual world, the truth is opposite of this. His cleanliness, his salvation with God, is not maintained according to the rules of natural cleanliness. It is maintained through prayer and is not affected by contact with others. In fact, cleanliness is spread from him to others through this contact and is made visible in healing. This is shown in the story of the hemorrhaging woman in 5:25–34. The bleeding woman is technically unclean according to God's law, and contact with her would also make Jesus unclean (Leviticus 15:25–27). But in Mark's story, the woman's contact with Jesus makes her clean, rather than making him unclean. So Mark radically rewrites the purity code by insisting that cleanliness is contagious.

Mark allows us to imagine a spreading wave of salvation, as the world is cleaned through the work of God. Revelation has little hope for a widespread salvation, and the walls between clean and unclean require constant vigilance. While this contrast may seem a bit abstract, it is key to our understanding of salvation. Are we speaking about the salvation of the world or about our salvation from the world? When we think about salvation coming from God, do we mean that God is at work in the world attempting to bring harmony and justice, or do we mean that God is at work trying to save us from his wrath that is coming on an unclean world?

70 AD

The writers of the New Testament generally agree that apocalyptic expectation was part of the message of Jesus. It is a consistent part of the earliest tradition. The exception may be the Gospel of John, although the letters of John contain a strong apocalyptic message (see 1 John 2:18). The most obvious problem here is that Jesus didn't do the task assigned to him by apocalyptic tradition. If his remaining task is to come as judge and king, he has thus far failed to show. So either Jesus was wrong or the early church misunderstood Jesus.

The more significant problem is that the apocalyptic message is inconsistent with the life of Jesus. If Jesus was really the Son of God, and if God is ultimately about power and might, then Jesus of Nazareth was a really bad image of his Father. He lived in a rather backward corner of the

New Testament—the bad news

world, unnoticed by the political and military rulers of the larger world. Even locally, he held no position of authority. He failed to call down fire and brimstone on his enemies, limiting himself to sermons proclaimed to peasants.

Jesus' more obvious displays of power were his miracles. The Greek word we translate as "miracle" means "act of power." These actions may have demonstrated his connection with God, but they failed to vault him into the realm of power. He healed the poor and the lowly rather than the powerful. When you compare his actions to the miracles of Moses, they are rather underwhelming. So either we need to admit that Jesus failed to bring salvation, or we need to take the life of Jesus seriously as a paradigm for salvation.

Besides the reality of the life and example of Jesus, any attempt to take "salvation" seriously must also deal with the events of 70 AD. About thirty-five years after the death of Jesus, the people of Galilee and Judea rebelled against their Roman rulers. This was one of a string of rebellions by the Jewish people in an ongoing attempt to free themselves from foreign rule. The one that took place in 70 was little different, except that, for the apocalyptic Jesus bunch, it must have looked like the culmination of all their dreams. This was the perfect time, the perfect place, and the perfect situation. If God was going to save his people, what better opportunity, what greater necessity, what more ideal conditions? The armies of Satan (aka the Romans) had surrounded the city of God, and were threatening the Temple of the Most High God. The faithful people inside Jerusalem were slowly starving to death as the Roman army surrounded the city and crucified anyone who attempted to escape. If God was ever going to do his power-and-might thing, this was the time. If Jesus was waiting for a moment to demonstrate to the whole world that he was truly coming to deliver his people, what better opportunity could ever present itself?

Then the Roman army broke a hole in the walls of Jerusalem, killed all the people inside, and destroyed the residence of God on earth. And God did nothing, at least nothing that fit the apocalyptic framework. Jesus decisively failed to appear to bring salvation. Apocalyptic Christianity survived this event. Since then, it has constantly survived a long series of failures. History is filled with near-perfect opportunities for God to fulfill the power-and-might salvation fantasies of Christians and equally filled with God's refusal to act in that way.

You Are Not Going to Heaven (and why it doesn't matter)

The apocalyptic tradition is an attempt to deal with the reality of Jesus' death while maintaining a belief in the God of power and might. If Jesus came to bring salvation, how is it that the people of God remained a persecuted minority in a world ruled by forces who actively opposed them? The New Testament was written in a world where hostile forces made the decisions, and the church was surrounded by people who were unaware, apathetic, or even hostile. In the experience of the New Testament writers, the purpose of the Roman army was to maintain the status quo, to maintain the rule of Satan in this world. Especially after the destruction of the temple, and in light of the ongoing, albeit sporadic, persecution of the church, it is not surprising that the early church looked for a paradigm of God working in the world that required decisive intervention from outside.

So apocalyptic thought grew logically out of their experience in the world as it clashed with their belief in salvation. Obviously Jesus' life and death failed to bring any catastrophic change in the world. The Messiah had come and proclaimed salvation, yet they remained a powerless and persecuted group. Within a system that proclaims belief in an all-powerful deity, nothing can have gone wrong. God cannot be said to fail. Yet the early Christian community remained a small, powerless minority, largely ignored by the world around it. The disjunction between the proclamation of salvation and the reality of the church created the need to which apocalypticism was a response.

This reconstruction of the early church highlights the gulf between the experiences of the early church and my experience as a middle-class North American Christian. I write as someone who doesn't need to be rescued. Alongside the gospel of Jesus Christ, I have been taught the gospel of self-sufficiency and the gospel of independence. As an educated person, I shouldn't need to be rescued. That would be a sign of my failure rather than a sign of God's victory. The early church was mostly filled with the poor and uneducated, those in need of rescue from the very real problems of hunger and oppression. It is no wonder their view of salvation was different from mine.

On the other hand, I do have history on my side. The God who failed to show up in 70 AD has also failed to show up in any other times and places where divine rescue would have come in very handy. This is not to say that God was absent in these events, but merely to note that the rescue-from-the-sky did not happen. So whatever salvation means, it must deal with this present-yet-absent God.

New Testament—the bad news

This does not make the answer any more obvious. It does, however, remove one of our options. If our understanding of salvation is based on an understanding of a God who reaches down from the sky to bring death and destruction on our enemies in decisive ways, we need to somehow find a reason why God has failed to do this since back in the exodus from Egypt. Alternately, we can hear the millions of other stories about the way God has worked in this world, and take them as indicative of who God is. We can also recognize the God of power-and-might as an extension of our own revenge fantasies and reach toward a theology that does not trap us in adolescent daydreams.

OPTION B—HEAVEN

One of the simple realities of dealing with salvation as a historical question is that this world does not conform to any picture of what salvation "should" look like. Whether the question is of the prosperity of the wicked or the continued suffering of God's people (i.e. any people), we continue to believe that a world that has been saved by God will look different from the way the world looks now. If nothing else, there should be some basic justice in a world where God is truly in control.

This leads to a number of possible responses. One way the church has reacted is to project the justice and faithfulness of God into heaven. If this world is not the place where the justice of God works itself out, and if God is truly loving and just, then this justice must be enacted in another plane of existence. Heaven becomes the place where God rewards those who have been faithful and where the blessings of orthodoxy can be seen.

In this framework, the reality of salvation becomes a hope. Christian expectation moves out of this world. Salvation, then, is all about rescue *from* this earth, not rescue *on* this earth. Yes, there may be partial rewards here on earth, but the big reward is moved out of the earthly plane. Like in the apocalyptic vision, Christian salvation focuses on the great Someday, but this someday is after death.

This picture of salvation does not really need to deal with the social and political realities of Jesus' life at all. It matters not at all who crucified Jesus or why. Jesus came to earth to die, which he did. This act is the way for us to get into heaven. Salvation only happens when we get to the right place after death. So Jesus' life was not a failure in bringing about the kingdom of God; rather, Jesus' life was mostly something that had to happen so he could die. He also had to tell us how to take advantage of his death, which becomes the core of our gospel message. All this is part of God's grand plan to get us into heaven.

Here is where atonement theology usually comes into the picture, attempting to explain why God can't just forgive us, why God would throw anyone into hell at all, and whether or not God really needs blood and death to be satisfied. This brings us back to the old focus on the *how* of salvation. After all, if the goal is to get into heaven, it becomes vitally important for us to know in advance whether or not we will succeed.

This is both the curse and blessing of focusing on heaven. The curse is that we can never know for sure, and once we're dead it's too late. There are no signs along the way that tell us we're on the right path. There is no physical manifestation that separates those going up from those going down. Do we need just to believe the right thing(s), and if so, what exactly are they? Can you get into heaven if you don't believe in heaven? Are actions also necessary? If so, which ones? How many sins are too many? Are some unforgivable? Or is attitude more important than actual actions (so long as you're trying . . .)? Or is it really just an arbitrary choice of God, and we're just stuck with that?

The curse is never knowing for sure (followed by an eternal discussion of whether we can ever know). But never knowing for sure is also the blessing. We can never disprove that the system works. Heaven is not subject to disproof. So we can continue to believe in the justice and faithfulness of God despite all evidence to the contrary all around us. We can also believe in the justice and faithfulness of God while continuing to participate in unjust systems here on earth. We do not need to think about systems at all because we are only concerned with the fate of individual souls.

So as a preacher, I can talk about heaven every Sunday in church, and no one can refute my arguments so long as my picture of heaven does not overtly contradict the descriptions in the Bible. There is still danger here, since the Bible does not have a single uniform description of the afterlife (and, in the minds of many, the Bible cannot contain contradictions). So there may be those in the congregation who know their heaven verses well enough to dispute with me, but in general I am safely in the realm of pure belief, unconnected to empirical reality. The world of belief is the creation of words, specifically the Word of God (here being the Bible rather than Jesus). We can argue about Bible verses, but it is unusual (though not impossible) to get into extended discussions about where in the sky heaven

New Testament—the bad news

can be found. In some significant sense, this is the postmodern dream, the world of pure signifiers without referents.

All this is necessary because some in the early and current church choose not to ground salvation in current human experience. In this case, however, it is useful to note that the New Testament actually has less focus on heaven than much of current Christian thinking. This often comes as a surprise to my students. They expect to study the New Testament to learn more about getting to heaven, but they find that it often has other goals in mind. This is especially true when they realize that the kingdom *of* heaven is not the kingdom *in* heaven.

If we begin again in Mark's Gospel, we find few references to heaven. For the most part, heaven is depicted as the abode of God (e.g. 11:10, 25). The voice at Jesus' baptism comes from heaven (1:11); Jesus looks up to heaven in prayer (6:41; 7:34); signs (8:11) and the baptism of John (11:30) come from there.

The only indication of a human future in heaven is 10:21. This is the story of the rich young man, who was exhorted by Jesus to store his treasure in heaven rather than on earth. This rather enigmatic sentence is open to a variety of interpretations. It is certainly possible to think that this treasure will be waiting in heaven for those who die, although this is not the only possible way to understand this verse. What we do learn from this brief study is that Mark has over 660 verses that are not about going to heaven, and only one that might indicate life after death as a major concern.

Luke offers us a picture of heaven that is basically the same as Mark's. The major new addition is that Jesus was carried up into heaven at his ascension. (24:51). Thus Jesus went up to the abode of God. Whether we as humans will also go to heaven to be with God at some point is not clear.

Matthew mentions heaven a lot more. This is because whereas Mark and Luke record Jesus as speaking about the "kingdom of God," Matthew regularly records this phrase as "kingdom of heaven." I find that my students often equate the kingdom of heaven with heaven itself, but this fails to make sense of a significant number of Matthew's references. If we equate kingdom of heaven with heaven, we need to believe that heaven has been taken by force by the violent (11:12), that an enemy has sown the weeds in heaven (the parable of the wheat and weeds, 13:24–30), or that heaven is small but growing (the parable of the mustard seed, 13:31–32). It may be possible to reinterpret these verses to make sense of them as references to heaven, but it is much more logical to understand them as references to the rule of God here on earth (an extension of "your will be done on earth as it is in heaven," 6:10).

Matthew also has more references to heaven as the abode of God. Jesus speaks often of God as a father in heaven (e.g. 6:26; 11:25; 12:50). He also adds numerous references to things that happen in heaven (angels see God's face in 18:10; things are bound in heaven in 18:18; the angels in heaven don't marry in 22:30). So heaven is the place where God lives, along with the angels. The question of humans or souls in heaven is less clear.

Matthew parallels Mark's reference to treasure in heaven (Matthew 19:19) and includes the idea of reward in heaven in 5:12 and a further reference to treasure in heaven in 6:20. So persecutions are endured (5:12) and treasures are stored up (6:20) for the eternal reward. Nothing directly is said here about heaven itself as a reward or as a place for justice, except that our reward is transferred there. This does imply, however, that the consequences of salvation can be moved outside the world. On the other hand, the dialogue with the Sadducees regarding marriage after the resurrection (22:23–33) does not directly state whether the resurrection takes place on earth or in heaven. It is most likely that both the Pharisees and Sadducees would have assumed that the resurrection would take place on earth, and Jesus did nothing to contradict them. Matthew's references to heaven, then, do not provide an unambiguous indication of a future salvation in heaven.

When the Gospel of John speaks about heaven, the most common phrase is "from heaven," usually speaking of Jesus' origin (e.g. 3:13, 6:38). One reference to a human future in heaven is, "I go to prepare a place for you" (14:2). This phrase is ambiguous, but it is easy to add "in heaven," making it a clear reference to our future with God. While this is only a minor point in John's otherwise complex gospel, it is easily latched on to by those who wish to move salvation out of our earthly existence. It is possible to counter this assertion by noting that John claims that God is already present with us, in the form of the Advocate (14:16), but it doesn't take a lot of self-examination to recognize that Jesus' presence with us does not always provide the expected rewards of life at one with God.

So if we look to Jesus as our guide in thinking about heaven, in general this means that we wouldn't think about heaven. Heaven is the abode of God, and things are fine there. Things happen in heaven, but these are not our problem. The kingdom of God is coming and/or already present among us, but this is an earthly reality. We should focus on lives rather than souls.

New Testament—the bad news

Given Paul's strongly apocalyptic bent, it would be surprising to find him interested in heaven as a reward. After all, if Jesus will soon return, what is the need of a reward in heaven? I realize that many people construct a hybrid system in which Jesus returns to take us to heaven, but this is unlikely to be Paul's picture. Paul most often talks about the *parousia*, the *unveiling* of the Jesus who is already with us. For Paul, Jesus is already present. The world does not see or understand this and so does not acknowledge Jesus as savior. Some day this already-present Jesus will be revealed/unveiled to all humanity. There is no need for a human future in heaven in this scenario.

The most obvious reference to reward in heaven is 2 Corinthians 5:1, 2, where Paul speaks of a heavenly dwelling prepared for us. A Paul scholar is likely to point out that the "tent" mentioned in 5:1 is our earthly bodies, which will be replaced by an eternal "heavenly" body at the return of Jesus. This still fits into Paul's general framework of Jesus' return to this earth, while dealing with the problem of being part of the kingdom while our bodies continue to suffer and die. Paul paints a picture of ourselves with new bodies, ones not corruptible. It is likely that he sees these bodies as dwelling on earth with Jesus. On the other hand, most readers of the Bible do not have Paul scholars readily available to them, so it would not be surprising for this verse to be used to refer to life after death in a heavenly place.

Other Pauline verses that refer to heaven include Philippians 3:14, where Paul speaks of a heavenly calling. This verse refers to a calling from heaven (i.e. from God), but again it is easy to read this verse to mean a heavenward calling (us being called to heaven by God). Colossians 1:5 (assuming for the moment that it is from Paul) speaks of a "hope laid up for you in heaven," which sounds quite similar to Jesus' words in Mark. Again, Paul is not clear whether this reward is waiting for us to retrieve, or whether Jesus will bring it for us at the second coming. The latter makes more sense of Paul's general thinking, but the former is available as an interpretation, especially at funerals.

The clearest reference Paul makes to continuing life after death is Philippians 1. In verse 10, Paul retains his apocalyptic framework by speaking of the coming "day of Christ," referring to the return of Jesus. But later in the chapter, he states that "my desire is to depart and be with Christ," while speaking of his own death. This is further complicated by 1 Thessalonians 4:16, which seems to imply that the "dead in Christ" (those who have died before Jesus' return) are currently still in their graves, awaiting the resurrection at the time of Jesus' return.

These few verses do give us some support for shifting the effects of salvation to a heavenly reward, but for the most part Paul preferred his apocalyptic scenario. While both act in similar ways, the heavenly reward plan is more easily digested today, given that we are still waiting for the *parousia* 2,000 years after the birth of Jesus. So in many churches today, Paul is loosed from his apocalyptic roots and planted in the fertile soil of life-after-death salvation.

There are a few other verses in the New Testament that speak of or at least imply that human unity with God has been moved to a postmortem existence. 1 Timothy 4:8 (which is generally believed to be written later by a disciple of Paul) speaks of a "life to come." Hebrews 11:16 mentions a heavenly country and a heavenly city. 1 Peter 1:4, again sounding like Jesus in Mark, talks of "an inheritance kept in heaven for you," and 2 Peter is expecting the destruction of the current heaven and earth, while waiting for new ones (3:7–13), but the mention of a new earth suggests that the writer believes the natural dwelling place of humans is on earth.

This picture of a new heaven and a new earth is echoed in Revelation (21:1). This allows for a hybrid picture, where the outworking of salvation is both after death and earthly/apocalyptic. So while not all of us can expect to witness the coming of Jesus, the destruction of the current earth suggests at least some interim time (possibly in heaven) for Christians, with a final apocalypse to follow.

So the New Testament contains a variety of references to a life after death with God in heaven. Perhaps the most significant result of this study, however, is not the recognition that the New Testament contains a variety of scenarios for salvation outside history but to notice how little this question arises at all. The Gospel of John, for example, has twenty-one chapters about the possibilities and realities of salvation here in this life but only two verses that may move this gift to another plane of existence. Life after death in heaven may be the goal of most Bible tracts currently being printed, but it is a rather minor part of the New Testament picture of salvation.

CONCLUSION

If we are going to take seriously the idea that the gospel message of salvation offers us a way forward for life on this earth, we also need to be honest about the ways in which the Bible is not helpful. This is not meant to disparage the authors of the text. They were responding to the realities of life around them and the ongoing work of God among them. But their answers have proven unhelpful in bringing about a world where God's will is done, offering instead an escape from the challenges that confront us.

Yet still the temptation remains. There is a huge gulf between the world as it is and the world as God intended it to be. The task of bridging this gulf is monumental. Worse, the church has often been part of the problem rather than part of the solution. So the desire to escape from the challenge and instead give the problem wholly to God is a regular part of Christian life.

The New Testament offers us two forms of escape: apocalypticism and heaven. Both of these allow us to wait for some future event (Jesus' return or our death) where God will solve these problems without help from us. Both are also handy because they are incapable of being disproven. I can't prove that Jesus will not return tomorrow to destroy his (and my) enemies in flaming fire. Neither can I prove that heaven is not waiting as the place where justice is finally done, where God finally shows everyone who is good and who is bad, who is right and who is wrong.

Both of these forms are useful to church leaders because we can't ever know for sure (in an experiential way) whether we're in or out. So we need to keep coming to church to be reassured (or have our guilt recharged, which comes with its own reward system), which keeps the pastors and theologians employed. This also means that the organization of church does not need to organize anything except itself. Since it has no task except to exist, to spread or be the message to itself or others, it is self-perpetuating but not actually responsible for any change in the world around it. It has no standards to meet except existence or possibly growth.

On the other hand, most of the Bible is concerned with providing a way forward for life on this earth. The Exodus, apocalyticism and life-after-death are exceptions rather than paradigms. If we leave behind the trap of waiting for the big rescue-from-the-sky, we are confronted with a wide variety of tasks, goals, and offers of help from the God who is concerned about the world as it currently is. This way forward is not simple or singular. The Bible is not going to do all our thinking and planning and acting for us. But it may prove to be a vital companion on our journey. It is to this task that we now turn.

4

Old Testament—the good news

a) We're all in this together

When we look to the Old Testament for models of salvation that contribute to the long-term future of the earth, it is important to note where it begins. It begins by thinking about salvation communally. The Old Testament is dedicated to the survival and well-being of the people of Israel as a whole, rather than the survival or success of the individual.

In many ways, this idea of communal salvation is so obvious that it is easy to overlook. It is like breathing—you don't really notice it most of the time, but that doesn't mean you have stopped. Today we so easily read the Old Testament and assume it fits our modern individualistic perspective (if we read it at all). So it is jarring to realize that our modern notion of the "individual" is largely absent from the Bible. Each person is merely a unit within a larger family, clan and tribe. In this structure, individual survival is only important because individuals contribute to the well-being of the community. This perspective becomes obvious when we study specific parts of the Old Testament.

STORY

The story begins with one—one God. Yet even here, the single God does not speak this aloneness, but in the first self-reference speaks of "us" making humanity (1:26). So the first creation story makes it appear perfectly natural that the creature made in God's image is naturally two—male and female (1:27).

Even in the second story of creation (2:4–25), where the first human creature is single and alone, God is immediately distressed by this. God is concerned by its aloneness and creates first the animals (2:19) and then Eve, so that the human would not be alone. Within this context, the Fall is what happens when people make decisions without consulting the group. Eve chooses, making an individual decision that has consequences well beyond herself. Thus, one of the lessons of the serpent and the fruit is that you should never make decisions without talking to others who will be affected by your actions.

When we look to the Cain and Abel story, it is easy to see the group perspective. This is what happens when individual concerns override family. The story continues to emphasize the relationship between Cain and Abel. They are brothers (4:2, and six times in 4:8–11). The sin committed by Cain is not murder but destruction of family, the consequences of which are removal from family and the death that is likely to follow. Any person alone is considered a "fugitive and a wanderer" and loses the protection that family offers (4:14).

In most cases, this "we're all in this together" perspective is simply assumed rather than proclaimed. The story of Abraham is a good example. At first glance, it may look like the call of an individual. Abram, in fact, is called away from his family (12:1), but the promise that immediately follows is of the creation of a new people.[1] While this new people is only a future hope, even in the beginning Abraham is far from alone. He is an individual who operates as the head of a large group. When he sets out to follow, he is accompanied by his wife, Sarah, his nephew Lot, and "the persons whom they had acquired in Haran" (12:5). Reading on, we soon see that this number includes "trained men, born in his house, three hundred eighteen of them" (14:14). So even before the birth of his first child, Abraham is the leader of a sizeable group of people, all of whom are part of the covenant God offered to Abraham. When Abraham moved, they moved. When Abraham went hungry, they went hungry (possibly even hungrier). When Abraham prospered, they prospered.

---

1. The language becomes tricky here because English doesn't have good words for this. The "people" of Israel are a group beyond family, clan or tribe, but are not a "nation" in the modern sense. "Ethnic group" might work, but the root of "ethnic" also just means "people."

As the story continues, the number of people affected by the actions of their leaders and their God also continues to grow. The people survive together, go to Egypt together, go into slavery together, and escape slavery together. The story is not about a bunch of individuals who joined or didn't join a particular religion in order to go to heaven. Occasionally some people decided to be inside or outside the group, but these stories are more rare than common, and no mention is made about life after death. The decisions people made were about how they were going to live before they died, and these decisions affected them and the people around them.

So while we abandoned "Exodus" as paradigm for how God works because it was not a reflection on the real experiences of the Jewish community in the Persian period (see chapter 2), it still remains a paradigm for communal salvation. Yes, the story often focuses on a particular person, Moses, but his call is the salvation of an entire people. The people of Israel did not each decide to individually run off into the wilderness. They travelled together, ate together, went hungry together, and ultimately survived together.

The story of the people of Israel continues in a similar way. Some individuals are highlighted in the story—judges, kings and prophets—but the focus remains the overall salvation of the whole people of Israel. This salvation is understood in terms of faithfulness to covenant, justice, mercy, worship, and other components, but the message remains that the people of Israel are all in this together.

RITUAL

Outside the story of Israel, we can also see communal salvation in the various texts that describe and prescribe ritual. These include stories of ritual such as Exodus 12:14–20, laws about ritual in Leviticus and Numbers, psalms that fit within ritual, and prophetic texts that assume ritual settings (such as the temple) or ritual performance. All these rituals are grounded in tradition, the traditions of the people of Israel.

Rituals both create and reinforce community. Even rituals that describe the actions of an individual are set within a larger community. Take, for example, the ritual sacrifices assumed in Genesis 12:7, 8.[2] The text

---

2. The text only says that Abraham built an altar. It is the larger context of expectation that causes us to assume that Abraham sacrificed on these altars. The existence of this assumption itself embeds us within a larger social worldview.

merely says that Abraham "built an altar to the LORD and invoked the name of the LORD," and it assumes that we know what this would have looked, sounded, and felt like. We are likely to read this as the actions of one person, but it is much more likely that there is an entire community there to witness the event. Further, the story also creates expectation and a pattern to be followed. How should someone respond when God makes a promise? You build an altar (and presumably sacrifice). And how do you do that? You do it the traditional way, the way your parents did it, the way your entire community does it. In this sense, even the individual act of sacrifice reinforces your belonging to a particular community.

A whole host of texts affirm/enforce/reinforce ritual. Usually these are set within a social context, with the minimal requirements of altar and domesticated animals (and assume a system of village agriculture). More often priests, temples, and communities of participation and audience are assumed. In this way, texts create communities of action and participation. Over and over, the rituals reinforce or simply assume communal salvation. We are either going to survive together or we are not going to survive at all.

This remains true even when the rituals being described are not even performed. Even after the cessation of the ritual activities, the text remains as a substitute. We can see this clearly when we remember that, in the time of the writing of much of the Old Testament, after some of the people of Israel had returned from exile in Babylon, most of the "people of Israel" lived nowhere near Israel. And because the text does not allow sacrifice outside Jerusalem, most Jews cannot perform the actions required. What they can do instead is read the text. The ritual of reading the text makes it possible to be part of community even when physically remote.

VILLAGE AGRICULTURE

Another way to understand the communal nature of salvation in the Old Testament is to remember that this is a system based on cooperative agriculture. This is not the modern American understanding of the lone man with his wife and children living on the (mythic) family farm. The Old Testament assumes an extended family (parents, children, their children, plus accumulated and acquired family) living in a village, all of whom worked together for the common good. Yes, each extended family has specific land that is "theirs" (although ultimately everything belongs to God), but there are also the fields of common land for grazing, and the general recognition is that the village survives and prospers (or not) together. Rain does not fall on one field at a time. Plagues affect whole regions. Drought is often widespread, and animal diseases can infect whole herds.

In an agricultural system, survival of the community also means survival of the land. In this system, land is not raw material for exploitation but is part of the same system that includes humans and animals. The connection between the people, animals and land was much more obvious for them than it is for most of us. If you ruined the land, you went hungry. Much of the land was marginal at best. The "fair green hills of Galilee" are mostly rock, covered with little or no topsoil. Successful farming of this land was the result of generations of accumulated wisdom.

Growing enough food for continued survival, plus some "extra" for celebrations, feasts, and taxation, was difficult. It required the action of entire communities over decades and centuries. The various generations within a family worked together, along with the entire village, to ensure ongoing survival. In this system, "salvation" was the result of hard work, cooperation, and a multigenerational commitment to the health of the ecosystem. The village was either going to survive together or not at all.

COVENANT

Perhaps the most obvious indication of communal salvation is the centrality of covenant. This is one of these topics that is so large, it is easy to overlook. We might say that covenant is the forest, and the rest of these topics are the trees. Despite the widespread scholarly discussion on covenant, it is not easy to reconcile with our current worldview. Our individualistic culture does not easily think about generational treaties with God. Yet thinking in terms of covenant can also be very useful for the postmodern church. Covenant is the ultimate expression of "we're all in this together." The people of Israel as a whole come together to affirm their corporate relationship to God. Together they maintain the various institutions that focus their relationship to God.

It is also important to remember that, at its core, the Old Testament is a document that is foundational for an entire social structure. We too easily put it in the category of the "religious." We have this neat distinction between the sacred and the secular, and the Bible belongs in the first category. But the Old Testament was intended as the constitution for an

Old Testament—the good news

ethnic/political group and was meant to serve as the foundational language for their whole society.

This is an important distinction between their view of Scripture and ours. We place the Bible in the "religion" section of the bookstore (and our lives), setting it apart from the various other categories we operate with. But if there had been an ancient Israelite bookstore, the Torah would have been shelved under religion, law, social sciences, parenting, and nearly every other category in the store. It was their constitution, not just their moral code.

What makes the concept of covenant challenging for many today is that, as a legal system, the enforcement of the Law is ultimately based on the belief that God punishes groups for the sins of the group. This makes sense only if you really believe that God punishes groups, and if you are ready to categorize political, military, or natural occurrences as truly "acts of God." This is quite a stretch for many people. We only need to remember the protests from a wide variety of groups when certain Christian leaders tried to call the events of 9/11 or Hurricane Katrina the punishment of God for specific sins. Or think about your response when you hear that the Westboro Baptist Church from Topeka, Kansas, regularly protests at military funerals because they connect the deaths of soldiers with the American acceptance of homosexuality. However repulsive we find these examples, these are both examples of people willing to connect horrible acts with the punishment of God.

Part of our reaction to the above examples is to the sins that are chosen for condemnation by these groups. But this only clarifies the difficulty of making a connection between certain acts of the group and other events that are not directly related. In the Old Testament, the stories and the prophets regularly make direct connections between things that have no obvious natural connection. Incorrect worship leads to plague (Exodus 32:35). Worshiping other gods leads to political decline (2 Kings 17:7–23). Injustice in the court system leads to being conquered by a foreign army (Micah 7:3). The connection between sin and punishment does not follow an understanding of the natural consequences of human action and so is always subject to debate and disagreement.

On the other hand, this is no longer the problem we face. For the most part, there is a fairly straightforward connection between human actions and the larger problems facing our world. While there remains a discussion about the details or the solutions, the larger problems facing our world arise directly from identifiable causes. Global climate change comes from carbon dioxide. Wars come from people shooting at each other. Species disappear because of loss of favorable habitat. Yes, somewhere in all this God is at work, but God generally appears disinclined to rescue us from our own stupidity and destructiveness.

Within this scenario, covenant is the recognition that actions have consequences and that these consequences affect entire communities. Thus, the notion of covenant gives us a framework for the community to restrict the actions of the individual. We as a human community, and more locally we as a nation/state/town/family, have a covenant that includes all of us and the whole earth (not just the people on it). This covenant puts us in a symbiotic relationship with all of creation. The particular covenant in its local form may or may not include a particular deity or religious structure. It also does not require a particular individual to accept any religious creed or confession. The actions of a Christian who lives within a largely Buddhist region still affects the people of the region, whether or not they can agree on the ultimate nature of the universe. What the notion of covenant offers the church is a pre-existing framework for such an understanding. We don't need to reinvent the wheel; what we need is to see how the wheel helps us solve our current problems.

TEXTS

Another major indicator of the biblical idea of communal salvation is the existence of the Bible itself. Texts are produced in communities by communities for communities. People seldom write books for themselves. They also never write books by themselves. This is even truer in our modern world than it was in the ancient world.

Today we usually think about books and other texts (including electronic ones) as mostly the product of a single individual. There is one person listed as the "author," and that person wrote the book in front of us. So I sit at my laptop and am writing this book on my own. Of course, this is a myth. I sit (on a chair I didn't build) at my laptop (which speaks of worldwide community of hardware and software development and production and distribution) while drinking my coffee (grown thousands of miles from my home, then processed, transported, and brewed by others), writing this document (which speaks of a wide community of scholars and churches and interested persons) that will then go through many hands (editors, typesetters, proofreaders) before arriving in some form (which speaks of paper production or electronic systems) with you. So my individual production is actually only a small part of a huge web of people and systems.

What makes this look so individualistic is my disconnection from all these people. I don't know the people who grew the coffee or made the table. I don't even know which country either came from. I also don't know how many of these things are done. So I am disconnected from both people and process. I can duplicate a wooden chair, but not a chrome and plastic one. I cannot even empathize with the many people who made this space possible because I do not understand what was done.

In the ancient world, all of this is much more transparent. The people who write may also need to make their own paper and ink. They are likely intimately connected to the food production systems that allow them to be fed while doing this. They can possibly name the various people involved in the entire production process, most of whom are biologically related to them. So ancient text production was actually more individualistic than is our own. While the ancient author could likely make parchment and ink, my ability to create a laptop from raw materials is limited. Imagine being handed a pail of sand and being asked to create a silicon chip.

Even in the ancient world, however, the community was needed for a whole range of things. At the most basic level, the existence of language required community. In an ancient oral culture (where most people had no use for writing), the production of texts assumed an entire subculture of scribes who were usually linked to a temple and/or a government. This further implies a taxation system to support the "nonproductive" activity of the scribes.

A further sign of the communal nature of textual production is the way most of the biblical texts are unsigned. Who wrote most of the books of the Old Testament? The books of the prophets are most easily ascribed to an "author," but even these texts were written, copied, and maintained by a group other than the prophets themselves. In this sense, these were "our" texts.

Further, the continued existence of these texts over millennia speaks to a community of collection and maintenance. After all, how many other texts survive from 2,500 years ago? How many nameless people were involved in the preservation of the Bible throughout the ages? This again reinforces the way the Bible is formed, written, and preserved by a community for the needs and uses of that community, rather than by an individual to promote some sort of individual salvation.

It is true that many of the psalms talk about individual salvation. Various psalmists call out to God for salvation from a variety of things (e.g. Psalms 7, 31, 54 and others). These are often classified as individual salvation psalms. What is interesting in these cases is that the writer's notion of salvation is equivalent to survival. This, too, is part of communal salvation. After all, communities do not survive if its members have died. So in the individual salvation psalms, the salvation requested is from famine, plague, war, or enemies, even from death in general.

EXTENDING SALVATION

While the survival of the community inside its covenantal relationship with God remains the primary goal for most of the Old Testament, this goal is often set within a larger context. Often this communal notion of salvation extends outward. The story begins with a worldwide focus in creation, flood and other stories of the human community. The story from Abraham forward is focused on a small group in the larger world, but part of the call is to be a blessing to the whole world (Genesis 12:3).

The book of Isaiah provides the most obvious example of the wider view of its vision. It starts local (chapter 1), with the problems and concerns of Judah and Jerusalem. But it quickly moves beyond these local concerns and becomes global in scope. Isaiah 2:1 is about Judah and Jerusalem, but 2:2 speaks about shifts in geography and thus includes the natural world in its vision for the future. This verse also speaks about "all nations," which further expands the vision to include all people, so that by 2:4, peace is established in the whole world.

In extending the idea of salvation beyond the people of Israel, the blessing of God is made concrete in the historical transformation of the world. This blessing is not about pie-in-the-sky spiritual salvation but a spirituality grounded in the reality of survival and prosperity.

In thinking about this, we need to continue to focus on the postexilic community. Prior to the exile, the Babylonians killed thousands of individuals as they raided the countryside and captured the cities of Israel. But despite all this destruction, they failed to kill "Israel." Thousands were taken off into captivity in Babylon, but for the exiles this meant the survival rather than the end of "Israel." Even the return from exile was only symbolically important rather than crucial for the survival of "Israel." In all this, individuals were relatively unimportant.

The movement of "Israel" from the region of Judea/Jerusalem to Babylon, Egypt and beyond also meant that the notion of "salvation" was expanded. Now the safety and survival of a small piece of geography was less crucial than the safety and survival of people scattered throughout much of the Mediterranean world and beyond. The situation in Babylon or Alexandria or Damascus or Rome was also part of the Jewish notion of "salvation." Suddenly the "we" who are all in this together included vast groups of people in far-flung cities and villages, since the security of the Jewish population in these places was connected to the security of the city and region.

INCORPORATING SALVATION

We often miss this notion of we're-all-in-this-together because it is assumed by the writers and readers in the ancient world. They didn't need to explain it because everyone already knew that. We miss it because we don't already know it. Instead we transpose these texts into our world of individual salvation.

Once we see it, it is also important to recognize how much unlearning this would take in most churches. Individual salvation rules. For us this idea is so natural that we don't need to explain it, it just is. When we start to look for it, it is easily seen in many places. Evangelism is understood as one person making an individual decision that affects their "personal relationship to Jesus" (a phrase found nowhere in the Bible). Numerical church growth is seen as a sign of health and the work of God, but why would this matter if we are truly all in this together? Even if we would divide the world into "those who are part of the problem" vs "those who are part of the solution," we are still all in this together. The idea of communal salvation challenges many of the basic ideas of what it means to be a "Christian." This would not be a simple change.

What would it mean to be "evangelical" if a particular belief system became only a small part of a larger transformation, a transformation that included the entire earth? What would it mean to be "Catholic" if we could recover its original definition of "universal"? These movements are certainly already at work in these and other groups. At every point, we need to challenge one another to think bigger—beyond the individual, beyond the social, beyond the religions, and beyond the human (remember the mosquitoes).

Much of the North American notion of what it means to be a Christian is wrapped up with modernist ideas of what a "religion" is. In the classes I teach at a university, my students expect Bible courses to be about "spiritual" things. They are comfortable with, "Give to the emperor the things that are the emperor's, and to God the things that are God's" (Mark 12:17) so long as God is willing to stay within the confines of the "religious." But communal salvation does not allow this neat secular/sacred division.

Incorporating this communal salvation into our postmodern worldview is important because, in a shrinking world, it is becoming ever more true. Pollution in China causes melting ice in Antarctica, which leads to flooding in Chile. War in Syria causes strife in Cleveland. A marriage in India lessens family conflict in Toronto. Politics in Kansas affect labor relations in Thailand. If our Christian faith has nothing to say to these realities, then we need to simply admit that we have divorced religion from reality, and God has abandoned the world.

THE DANGERS OF COMMUNAL SALVATION

A problem quickly becomes obvious when we study the Old Testament regarding communal salvation. Too easily this becomes an issue of group identity, where "my community" needs to be distinguished from "theirs." Israelite identity was forged by distinguishing the children of Abraham from a whole variety of other groups. Even within Abraham's lifetime, the "true" children of Abraham distinguished themselves from Abraham's "other" children, namely the descendents of Ishmael (Genesis 21:10). The list of "others" soon grew to include the Canaanites, Edomites, Egyptians, Philistines, Arameans, and so on.

As we saw in chapter 2, sometimes these distinctions were illusions. But at other points the distinction was unavoidable, when "they" were trying to kill "us" (and vice versa). Immediately after the Exodus, the Egyptian army attempted to recapture the fleeing Israelites, and there was little room for "can't we all just get along?" Later the Israelites attempted genocide on the Canaanites and were forbidden by God from getting along. So both sides enforced strict us/them distinctions, and there was no point in pretending these divisions did not exist.

Old Testament—the good news

Interethnic violence continues to be the reality in many parts of the world and is unlikely to disappear anytime soon. As more and more people compete for fewer and fewer resources, communities define themselves and work together. But what do we do when the salvation of us means the death of them? Can humanity survive this sort of ethic?

Here we see the possibility that the ancient Jew/Canaanite/Philistine distinctions are merely replaced by the modern American/German/Brazilian, white/black/brown or Christian/Buddhist/Atheist distinctions. These patterns of thought are already well-ingrained in our society and do not need further biblical encouragement. We see them in doctrines like American Exceptionalism and in the patterns of racism and religious bigotry that continue to be factors in the world today.

Another danger of this attempt to think communally about salvation is the simple fact that we can't go back. It doesn't work to try to impose a completely foreign sociological system onto a postmodern society. It might be possible to try to think this way ourselves and to raise our children like this, but this carries the risk of the church becoming (or remaining?) a quirky subculture that doesn't have much to say to the world because it doesn't speak the same language. How can we claim that "we're all in this together" when we refuse to integrate into the society around us?

Obviously this is a much larger issue that has no simple, single solution. I see this regularly in my classroom. I have students who have been raised with a "biblical," premodern worldview and who therefore don't really fit into their own culture. I also have students who have been raised to "fit" but as a consequence don't see how the Bible challenges many of their common assumptions. And the answer is not some easy middle ground. But here, perhaps the notion that "we're all in this together" can provide a place to begin the discussion. The goal of this discussion would be the larger benefit to the whole community, rather than fixing the ideas of a particular individual. In this, however, we cannot assume that "we're all in this together" is the right answer to which all must subscribe.

Another possible danger to the idea of communal salvation is that it can so easily sound (and become) Pollyannaish. There are many possible responses to this idea that do not recognize the real problems that exist in the world. "Can't we all just get along?" Just a few more pages of reading this book, maybe a discussion about it, and then we can gather around the campfire for a multilingual sing-a-long. Or not. Many people would be glad to work toward this great human community so long as it doesn't threaten their middle-class lifestyle. Once I read an article that called for a great movement of Christian unity, but only under the authority of the Pope. The list of foolishly optimistic notions floating around the Internet is endless. Isn't communal salvation just another one of these?

In various ways, communal salvation can be transformed into a naïve or even destructive force. This will become even more likely as more and more people compete for the limited resources of the earth. Communal salvation can become the survival of "us" at the expense of "them." Or it can be a nice dream that allows us to avoid the harsh realities of the survival of life on our planet. "Biblical" fantasies are still fantasies.

STILL

Whatever drawbacks or weaknesses there are in the idea of communal salvation, it remains much better than individualism. Individualism is a myth and a dangerous one. It invites disconnection between action and consequences. How can your water be clean when I dump toxins on the soil? How can you prosper when I don't pay you what your labor is worth? Whatever answers the church provides for itself and the world around it, it either begins with the idea that we are all in this together or it faces the real possibility of having nothing relevant to say.

Here the Old Testament provides a common language for the church as it tries to understand and live out a community-oriented faith. The framework and stories it provides show us another way forward. Israel survived or thrived as a people, and so do we. While we cannot simply import these ideas into a postmodern, diverse culture, we can use them as guides.

We are all part of communities in one way or another. There are very few true hermits. So there will naturally be some sort of definition to a group. If nothing else, there are people we know well and people we don't know at all. And if there is an us, then there must be a them.

But our postmodern overlapping "us's" transforms attitudes towards "thems." In leaving behind the idea of a single, stable individual identity, we move toward a notion of an us without fixed boundaries, which also destabilizes the identities of them.

For example, I have two friends who are very much part of the postmodern generation. He is a Hispanic American, born in Peru but raised in Los Angeles. She is Japanese, also raised in Los Angeles but with immigration issues that keep her from American citizenship. They recently got married in a combination Japanese/Peruvian/American/Christian wedding. If they have children, they will be American but also part of numerous other ethnic/national groups.

Further, while both of them are Christians, he (not she) comes out of Buddhist traditions, has significant Catholic influences, but has also been significantly involved in both black and Hispanic churches. He brings these ideas into his faith. Her background is more American megachurch. They are currently attending a small Mennonite congregation.

In all of this, who is us? If their notion of us includes all of these groups, it also must recognize that there are many within all these groups that would not accept them. And if I include them within my us, this does not make me Japanese or Peruvian, but it also does not allow me to lump these groups together as "outsiders."

This example also appears simple when compared with the complexity of community made possible by the Internet. What does it mean to participate in multiple, overlapping communities without getting out of bed? This new postmodern community won't be like the idea of community in the Bible, but it also won't fit the modernist notion of the rugged individual. Something new is emerging. Or rather, many new things are emerging. Whatever happens, the world is much more likely to increase in interconnectivity than decrease in it.

It is also sobering to note that the focus on communal salvation has a parallel in the reality of communal destruction. Yes, the human race could end and could be responsible for its own demise. This has been true since the nuclear age, but now it is true even without someone pushing a button. All we need to do is keep doing things the way we are, and the ecosystem that sustains us will change in unpredictable and likely very negative ways.

This also means that change must take place on a massive scale.

b) Contentment

YES, SALVATION IS COMMUNAL, but that doesn't answer what salvation looks like. Is it simply a matter of the survival of sufficient numbers of people? Is survival of the society itself also important? Or is it about something more than mere survival?

Before we can get to the answer of what salvation might look like, it is helpful to look at some of the motivation, some of the attitudes and drives that will help us reach this goal. In the Old Testament, the goal is partly just survival, but basic survival can come in a number of ways and be accompanied by different emotions and drives. As usual, there is no simple, single answer, but a significant part of the answer is contentment. Contentment is one of the signs that salvation has been achieved and is also one of the things that must happen before we can get there. This means that a lack of contentment means salvation still awaits.

Lack of contentment can come from various things. Injustice and greed can both produce discontentment. Some people have almost nothing yet are content. Others have everything they need and much more yet are discontent. So we need to understand roots of contentment in Old Testament and the ways it can be helpful for the world today.

AGRICULTURE

It is important to begin by remembering that the Old Testament works within a largely agricultural system. This is hardly surprising, given the realities of life in that time and place. The area we know as Israel/Palestine had few opportunities for survival beyond farming. There were no mineral resources (the promise of Deuteronomy 8:9 notwithstanding), no major ports, and no large rivers for the transportation of goods. There were a few minor trade routes, but these appear to have had little impact on the economy of the region. This means that there were few avenues for the accumulation of wealth beyond the accumulation of farmland. Imagine that the New York Stock Exchange only lists one company- Farm Inc. You can invest in Farm Inc. or not, but it's the only game in town.

Within this agricultural system, there was also a wide variety of types of land. As someone who lives in Kansas and has traveled to Israel and the West Bank, I can say that there is little land in Israel that Kansans would consider prime farmland. Much of the "land flowing with milk and honey" is marginal at best, with considerable effort and knowledge needed to scrape sustenance from the rocky hills and valleys.

Economically, this means that the accumulation of land does not necessarily mean that one is rich. If the land only produces enough for the many people needed to farm it, there is little "surplus" left for the "landowner." So traditionally, whatever the various laws or powers that governed the land, much of it was best left in the hands of small villages whose members farmed according to practices that had ensured survival over the centuries.

The other important factor in this economy is to recognize the difference between the villages and the cities. The village was the central unit of production. Most people lived in villages. People in the villages farmed the land around them, with extended families owning certain plots, while other areas were understood to be common land, available for grazing and use by anyone in the village. Each village was also almost entirely self-sufficient, with various people in the village able to make or fix whatever needed making or fixing while also all being involved in farming.

The cities, by comparison, were mostly nonproductive. Aside from those farming the land immediately around the city, the rest of the people in the cities contributed nothing of economic value to the society. Thus, in order to survive, they needed somehow to extract produce from the villages around them. They may have thought of this extraction as piety (gifts to God that just happen to be consumed by the priests and temple officials) or as taxation (tribute given to the rulers because of their sheer wonderfulness). This system is reflected in the Bible in places such as 1 Kings 4:22–23, where the daily provisions for Solomon's household are mentioned (thirty cors [180 bushels] of choice flour, and sixty cors of meal, ten fat oxen, and twenty pasture-fed cattle, one hundred sheep, besides deer, gazelles, roebucks, and fatted fowl) as if the extraction of this amount of resources from the surrounding countryside was a good thing.

This system also meant that the people in the villages mostly wanted to be left alone. In many cases, they likely did not care who was "king" except where it affected the amount of tribute demanded. This sociopolitical structure accounts for the libertarian streak that runs through the Old Testament (keeping in mind that it was a communalist libertarianism, rather than an individualist one). In this setting, libertarianism is the argument for less government, lower taxation and more local control over local affairs. It was in the best interest of the villages to be free from any control by the cities, since taxation meant that needed resources were flowing out while no services were provided in exchange.

This system of village subsistence agriculture is reflected in many parts of the Old Testament. Many of the laws simply assume agriculture as "the system," rather than as one option among many for making a living. There are no laws that regulate mining or interstate trade or port activities. Rather, they speak of land use, theft of animals, harvests and the sharing of them, and the general realities of village life.

This background of village agriculture provides for the modern middle-class reader a starkly different approach to life. It shows an approach to life where subsistence was thought of as a worthy goal. It was a world where enough was enough. Why do you need more than enough? And the threshold for declaring "enough" was no more or less than what it took to survive, with a small amount of surplus for festivals and celebrations. In this way, contentment was built into the social system rather than being an individual emotion.

The idea of subsistence is reflected in many passages, but again it is more assumed than proclaimed. There are few major passages extolling the virtues of subsistence farming, at least in a tone that suggests it as an unusual attitude. Instead, texts celebrate the life where the offer of "each one of you will eat from your own vine and your own fig tree" (2 Kings 18:31) is considered a sufficient reason to support one ruler over another (even a foreign one). The law assumes farming as the occupation of basically everyone, with the protection of land rights being a central concern.

Another place where this idea of contentment becomes clear is the whole idea of being satisfied. The Hebrew word translated "satisfied" is *sb'* and is based on the same root as the word Sabbath, which is also the same root for the number seven (so Sabbath means seventh day). Thus in Hebrew, the number for satisfaction, the number that represents sufficiency and completeness is seven. While this at first only appears mildly interesting, it is helpful to contrast our own society where the general number for sufficiency is more like one million (assuming that our society has any concept of "enough" at all). In popular culture, it is much easier to think of examples of people wanting a million dollars than those who desired or were satisfied with seven.

The Old Testament notion of contentment arises from within a notion of limited good. This means that there is thought to be a limited amount of resources in the world, and if someone has more than their share, then others must have less. This makes perfect sense in an agricultural system, where land is in limited supply. What it also means is that, while some might still envy the wealthy, it is also possible to see them as stealing from the poor. This idea is reflected in many passages such as Psalm 37:16, which proclaims the aphorism, "Better is a little that the righteous person has than the abundance of many wicked."

This idea of contentment is found in many (though not all) parts of the Old Testament. The law assumes an agricultural system where the land provides sufficiency for everyone, so the basis of social equality is that everyone owns land but no one owns a lot of land. Thus the Jubilee year provides a mechanism to return ancestral land to everyone, which also means that any large landowners will lose their estates (see Leviticus 25 and 27).

The Psalms also proclaim the attitude of contentment. Psalm 23, perhaps the most well-known passage in the Bible, begins with a confession of contentment, where we recognize that we "shall not want." Whether we understand this phrase as a hope for the future, a claim for the present or a hedge against greed, it is unlikely to lead to any sort of hyperconsumerism. It is, of course, always possible to find consumerist desire almost anywhere, so that we might find our many desires validated in the image of the overflowing cup (verse 5), but this requires us to really stretch the foundational image of a sheep lying in green pastures.

The wisdom literature in the Old Testament also provides many examples of contentment as foundational. Proverbs 30:8 proclaims " give me neither poverty nor riches; feed me with the food that I need." Many other proverbs extol the virtue of being satisfied with what one has. Ecclesiastes is the more obvious example, where the preacher expends much time and energy in accumulating wealth and power, then admits, "Then I considered all that my hands had done and the toil I had spent in doing it, and again, all was vanity and a chasing after wind, and there was nothing to be gained under the sun" (2:11). Finally, after searching for joy and contentment in many things, he concludes, "So I commend enjoyment, for there is nothing better for people under the sun than to eat, and drink, and enjoy themselves, for this will go with them in their toil through the days of life that God gives them under the sun" (8:15). Yet he does this with strong warnings against greed and acquisition, which are condemned as "vanity" and "a grievous ill" (6:2).

In all of this (and more), we see also that the opposite of contentment is greed. Greed is what keeps people from being content themselves and what destroys the contentment of others. Greed is discontentment because that is what it is. Greed cannot lead to contentment any more than overeating can lead to being satisfied.

In these and many other passages, the Old Testament provides for the creation and maintenance of a socioeconomic system that provides sufficient resources for everyone. Its promise, however, resembles President Hoover's "a chicken in every pot" more than it does the proclamation that

You Are Not Going to Heaven (and why it doesn't matter)

God wants us all to be rich. It is more about reward for hard work than about the dream of freedom from work.

It is also important to remember that it is a system. It is not a set of rules for the individual that will automatically lead to contentment. Rather, it requires contentment as a starting place. If everyone is satisfied with "enough," then there will be enough for everyone. This provision of enough comes not from a central administration like the temple or king, but both must work to maintain the system by doing justice.

Note also that this is not a complete system. Like much of the Old Testament, the text provides us with general guidelines. It seems to recognize that there will be regional variance. This is simply true in a region like Palestine. Topographical/geographical variation leads to sociological variation. What works in Bethlehem may not work along the shore of the Mediterranean or the shore of the Sea of Galilee. What works in the northern hills will not work in the southern hills. So the basic principles are provided and need to be applied at a local level.

What we are offered is the basic outlines of a world where people are content to live their lives. What they want from the outside world is to be left alone. They want to be left alone not out of fear or xenophobia but because they already have what they need.

Contentment, then, arises out of the recognition that the desire for more (greed) destroys the socioeconomic system put in place by the people's covenant with God. When we believe that we will be content once we have certain things, we have already moved away from contentment.

Note also that the basics here are very basic: water, land, and animals. If we have those things, we can make the rest. The other thing needed is freedom—from disease, drought, plague, famine, and war. This is not the vague "I can do anything I want" freedom of consumerist individualism. This is simply a freedom from things that get in the way of normal, successful farming practices.

This also means that contentment is a difficult thing to pull off in a modern society. Our current economy is based largely on consumer spending and overspending, which is driven by advertising, which promotes discontentment. There is no larger system that promotes and rewards contentment. There is also no parallel to the agricultural village of the ancient world. The people living in my small town often own significant pieces of land around their homes, and spend hundreds or thousands of dollars and hours annually maintaining this land, but mostly that is for growing lawns and gardens with no economic return. This is not wrong, but it simply recognizes that transferring the Old Testament system of contentment to the modern world is not straightforward.

The church, however, does or can have a role to play in making contentment a viable orientation. To begin, we need to recognize the way religion helps maintain the current system. In the pop culture version of Christianity, God is Santa for adults. This God wants to give us stuff. What God wants to give us is determined by what we think we lack. God can give us physical stuff (homes, cars, money), psychological stuff (peace, joy, love, and, yes, contentment) and/or spiritual stuff (salvation).

In this system, the ultimate consumerist vision is heaven. Heaven acts as a reward for being good (fitting in with consumerist society) and vision for the way things should be (where the streets are paved with gold and no one has to work). Thus heaven becomes the ultimate expression of capitalist desire. We want more stuff, and God will someday provide. The desire for reward and the dream of limitless abundance is foundational for both capitalism and heaven-focused Christianity. Someday we (or God) will create the perfect society, where work is rewarded and everyone can have more than they need.

In this form, Christianity becomes the religion of discontentment, where we are told that God wants us to have everything, and if we don't, there must be something wrong with us. So we need to keep coming to church so that we can get the stuff (physical/spiritual/psychological) that confirms our acceptability to God. While here on earth we will always have needs, someday Santa God will take us to the North Pole/heaven where all our desires will be fulfilled.

Few churches actually proclaim this. This is pop Christianity, not the faith of most people who attend church regularly. The purpose of phrasing things this starkly, however, allows us to see the way consumerism can infiltrate the church. It also reminds us that the proclamation of contentment is not an automatic part of Christian faith. Contentment can also become another consumer need, one more thing to add to our list of things we don't have yet.

THE DANGERS OF CONTENTMENT

Besides the reality that it can become another part of individualist consumer society, there are other sides of contentment that we need to look out for. These are outlined in the Old Testament, sometimes as warnings, but sometimes as traps that the writers themselves have fallen into.

The first danger is to desire contentment for ourselves but not for others. We're okay; everyone else is on their own. This can be true both communally and individually. Individually, we see this in the story of Abraham. Abraham left his family and traveled. While he did this as a response to the call of God, this had consequences for many people around him. If he left home and family behind, it is quite possible that many of his servants also did. His wife had to pretend she was his sister and become the wife of another man. Hagar and Ishmael faced the real possibility of starvation because Abraham needed to keep peace at home.

Another situation of individual contentment is found in many stories of the kings. The kings of Israel required provisions for their huge households and for their soldiers, but nothing is said in the Grand Narrative about the effect of this on the villages of Israel. Soldiers were sent here and there to expand the king's territory, and nothing is said of their suffering or the families they leave behind. Women were given and taken as wives and servants, but their pain is generally not recorded.

On a larger scale, the soldiers and civilians of the enemy are not mourned, even though they had little to gain from victory and much to lose from defeat. So the people of Israel could be content with their victories, but in a war there are always more losers than winners. So contentment can easily become the reward for oppression, where someone is satisfied only at the expense of another.

Another danger of contentment is that it can itself become a tool of oppression. It has been used by generations of slave bosses and managers to explain to underpaid workers why they should not rebel. "Eat, drink, be content with your work." While this message comes through much more clearly in parts of the New Testament (see Titus 2:9), it is also subtly present in parts of the Old Testament. So the poor are content in their poverty, the wealthy are content in their wealth, and occasionally the wealthy should share some of their excess with "those less fortunate," but nothing is said about the disparity itself.

This is most easily seen in the stories of the patriarchs. Abraham is wealthy, with many animals and other possessions. Of course, many of his possessions are people, in the form of slaves (e.g. Genesis 14:14, 15). The translators of the Bible prefer to call these people "servants," but they apparently are owned by Abraham and have no say in killing or being killed

Old Testament—the good news

in battle. This makes them slaves by most definitions of the word. We usually read these as wonderful stories of God's blessing on Abraham, without taking into account the people who actually do the work without receiving the reward.

Even more, wealth in general can be seen as a "blessing from God," as a reward for hard work and godliness. This implies that the poor are lazy and less godly. In this scheme, contentment can only come from wealth because it is a reward from God. This further implies that the poor cannot be content but must put their noses to the grindstone and work for the reward of contentment. Thus "contentment" becomes a further encouragement to participate more fully in the discontent that is the basis of capitalism, an (illusory) reward that comes only after years of hard work and striving for success.

A rather different perspective on the dangers of contentment comes to us in the Law. In a number of places, Deuteronomy warns that contentment can lead to forgetting God. So 6:10-12 talks about the problem of getting to the promised land, acquiring houses, vineyards and olive groves, and subsequently (or consequently?) forgetting God and serving other gods (v. 14). And while Deuteronomy 8:10 talks about being satisfied ("sevened") with all the things God has given, the following verses warn against forgetting God and failing to keep God's commands. A similar idea is echoed in 11:15-17, where the possibility of being satisfied and worshiping other gods (and therefore not following the Law) is accompanied by a threat of punishment.

This perspective makes sense in the Old Testament, where God is known through action. So the people lack something, and God provides. By extension, if the people can do things for themselves, God is no longer necessary. This is rather easy to see in our society, where we are able to do more and more for ourselves, and being independent is a major goal. So doctors provide healing, science provides answers for ultimate questions, the government provides aid in times of need, and we can make our own wealth, so God's role is limited to "spiritual stuff."

The final danger of contentment is that it can easily be just another "need" to be satisfied by consumerism. Capitalism would respond almost instantly. A movement of contentment would result in a market flooded with contentment books, magazines, wall hangings, and throw pillows. T-shirts about contentment would give way to entire lines of contentment clothing (with new styles arriving daily!). It is already a significant niche market and would only expand with demand.

STILL

Despite these cautions, contentment is still the most revolutionary idea in this book. If the churches were filled with contented people, it would result in a complete restructuring of the world economy. Imagine what Walmart would look like if people were content. Would it exist at all? This is so revolutionary an idea that it is almost impossible to imagine it actually happening on a large scale.

But contentment is not about that. If we ask the question about whether it will become popular, we are still thinking from a capitalist perspective, which is inherently anti-contentment. It is not an idea we need to sell. It is not subject to statistical analysis or quantitative discussion. It is about our attitude toward life and our actions in bringing "enough" to the lives of others. There is danger in assuming that ideas are only good if everyone does them. That means we start with the desire to go along with the crowd, which is rooted in discontentment.

Even more than that, it is always helpful to understand that contentment is not best measured by emotional attitudes. While it is a feeling, our feelings are not the best way to determine whether contentment has been achieved. In the Old Testament, contentment was achieved by creating a system where everyone had enough. This system created the conditions of contentment. If people did not feel content within this system, that was not a sign that the system was broken, but that the person was broken.

The message of contentment needs to be constantly reinforced, because consumerism is. It requires the creation of communities of contentment, but communities that are not content with injustice inside or outside their communities. If we only achieve it as individuals, we will not achieve it at all.

c) The Genesis model

As we have seen, the dominant model for encountering and dealing with other peoples in the Old Testament is the Exodus/Joshua model. This model assumes that we are in a state of conflict with anyone outside our group and that their prosperity is a threat to our existence. Even their existence may be a threat to ours. Thus, we must leave Egypt and utterly destroy the people in Canaan or we risk disappearing as a people. Along the way we may meet people who are not a threat to our existence, so there we must minimize interaction (Numbers 25) and respond to any conflict either by turning away (Numbers 20:14–21) or with overwhelming force (Numbers 21, 22).

We have also noted that this is an odd attitude for the returning exiles. They had neither the authority nor the army to carry out these strategies, and would have risked the violent intervention of the Persians should they have attempted them. It is also easy to see how an attitude of ethnocentric xenophobia is unlikely to provide a way forward for our world today. This attitude leads easily to conflict and confrontation and leaves little room for cooperation and reconciliation. There is no empty land left for people to migrate to, so we will either learn to get along or continue to kill one another.

The book of Genesis provides another model for getting to and surviving in the "promised land" and a competing example for getting along with others. After all, while Exodus is a story about the exile without actually speaking about exile, the story of Abraham in Genesis is actually about someone coming out of the region of Babylon and traveling to Israel/Palestine. It is about the arrival of this group of people in the area they believed was given to them by God yet needing to share it with others. It is about the negotiation of power, land, and scarce resources without the direct, overwhelming intervention of God. In other words, the story of Abraham in Genesis is, in some sense, the story of the returning exiles. Of course, this should not be a surprise, for history is always about "us" in some sense. Whatever the details of the events being retold, the stories chosen and the way they are presented say a great deal about who "we" are or who we think we are.

You Are Not Going to Heaven (and why it doesn't matter)

WALKING THROUGH GENESIS

Genesis begins with the big picture, with the creation of the heavens and the earth. So we begin by thinking on a much larger scale than just ourselves and our problems. There is a larger context for our actions, a larger plan of God, and a broader scope to our vision.

Genesis also begins with two stories of creation, with two distinct understandings of who God is and who we are in relation to God and the world around us. The first story, in Genesis 1, speaks of an orderly world where God creates specific classifications of beings on specific days, with the creation of humans as the final act. The second story, running through Genesis 2 and 3, tells of a creation where God creates plants and animals in response to the needs of the humans. So already by the end of Genesis 3, we are aware that there is more than one perspective on the world, more than one plan, and more than one way to explain and understand the world around us. This is not "them" against "us," because we subscribe to various viewpoints even inside our group.

The story then continues with a number of conflicts. But again they are not us against them, but us against God (Genesis 3) and us against each other (Cain and Abel, Genesis 4). So the beginnings of conflict are not seen as anyone's fault but our own. We do not need an enemy outside our gates for sin and evil to disturb our lives. We are fully capable of that on our own.

The stories of Noah (Genesis 6–9) are long and detailed, with many themes worth pursuing. For the returning exiles, these may have been used as warning against violence (6:11–13), as a reminder that God also cares for the animals around them, or as a general counter-narrative to the worldview of the people around them. In this, there is also the assumption that God cares for the whole earth, not just for one particular group of humans.

The tower of Babel story (Genesis 11), certainly a reminder of the architecture of Babylon, also serves as a reminder that the division of people into language groups was not part of God's original intention. In all these stories, the readers are placed within the events of the whole of creation, where God works in places and with people that are not part of our group. So when we get to the stories of Abraham in Genesis 12, we understand this to be part of the larger context of God-at-work.

The stories of Abraham and Sarah and their family are too long and complex to go through in detail, but a few themes will add a lot to our understanding of another way forward for the human race. The stories begin with God's call of Abraham to leave his extended family and go to "the land

Old Testament—the good news

I will show you." Initially Abraham was not promised exclusive right to the land, although he is promised that he will become a "great people" (12:2).[3] Abraham went as a response to this call, but there is a larger purpose articulated here. Abraham was called to be a blessing to "all the peoples of the earth" (12:3). This mission implies a certain kind of relationship to other peoples. Abraham's offspring are unlikely to be a blessing to other nations through constant warfare or oppression. It is unlikely that extreme isolation or attitudes of superiority are going to result in this widespread blessing. So whatever this future blessing is going to look like in detail, setting out on a course of blessing assumes at least a predilection to get along with others.

This basic attitude shows itself often throughout the Abraham stories. Even after God declared the land to be ultimately belonging to Abraham's offspring (12:7), Abraham continued to act in a way so as to get along with the other people in the land. We see this in the stories of battle in Genesis 14. While the casual reader may have difficulty figuring out who is battling whom and why, it becomes clear that Abraham was living among a group called the Amorites, who were his allies (14:13). Abraham has also stayed out of the conflict until it directly involved his nephew Lot, and then only got involved to the point of rescuing Lot and people associated with him. So Abraham was not aggressively getting involved in increasing his own wealth or status at the expense of others.

A more curious example of Abraham's willingness to get along with his neighbors immediately follows, with the odd story of Melchizedek (Genesis 14:18-20). Melchizedek was king in (Jeru)Salem, and was a priest of God Most High (Hebrew—*El Elyon*). This designation for a god has not been used to this point in Genesis, so it is unclear whether we are to regard this as the same god as the one worshiped by Abraham. Yet Abraham not only accepted the blessing of this king (thus acknowledging his superiority) but also tithed to him (14:19, 20). So Abraham was willing to go to significant lengths to get along with others in the land, even after God has promised it all to his offspring. It is as if Abraham was saying, "I have my place and you have yours." Abraham even pleaded with God for Sodom and Gomorrah (18:16–33). While the destruction of those cities might have given Abraham more land for his use, he still valued the lives of those (evil) people more highly than did God.

---

3. The usual translation "great nation" is anachronistic. The Hebrew word is not necessarily related to a specific piece of geography nor a specific political formation.

You Are Not Going to Heaven (and why it doesn't matter)

The theme of "just getting along with others" continues in numerous stories. After Abraham got over his fear of Abimelech, king of Gerar (ch. 20), he made a treaty with him (21:22–34). This may not seem significant, except when we remember that this will be strictly forbidden in Deuteronomy. This treaty was a specific response to a conflict over a well of water, a vital resource in that part of the land. So while Abraham showed that he was capable of going to war to protect his family, in most cases he preferred integrity and kindness (21:22, 23) which led to negotiation and exchange (21:30, 31).

A parallel story is also found in Genesis 26, where Abraham's son Isaac repeated the ruse of wife-as-sister because of his fear of Abimelech (apparently Abimelech is a bit slow), then again made a treaty with him after disputes over wells. While in general the parallels are striking, in this case when the disputes arise, Isaac moved his flocks (26:17, 22). So apparently one of the options for getting along includes backing off.

In all this, there remains a clear separation between Abraham and his family and the people of the land. Abraham (24:1–4) and Isaac (28:1, 2) were both insistent that wives for their sons must come from within the extended family rather than from neighboring people (this would have been the assumption in any case). Yet relations with these neighbors are characterized by negotiation and compromise. In this, there is the recognition that ethnic identities are not going away any time soon. Ethnic and racial differences will continue, but people can still get along. This can even be true in times and places where resources are scarce. Disputes will happen, but there are numerous ways to continue to live side-by-side despite this.

Although the stories of Abraham include instances of dispute with neighbors, the predominant conflicts are internal to the family. These include the quarreling between the herdsmen of Abraham and Lot (Genesis 13), the ongoing conflict between Sarah and Hagar regarding their sons (21), the rivalry between Jacob and Esau (27, 32), and Jacob's fear of his brothers-in-law (31). There is also the longer story of Joseph and his brothers (37, 42–45), which is interrupted by the efforts of Tamar to get justice from her father-in-law, Judah (38). So even within the stories of Abraham entering the "promised land," the real difficulties were those that happened inside the family. In these stories, it is not possible to blame "them" for the problem, and obviously devoting things to complete destruction (the option presented in Joshua) was not going to work.

Old Testament—the good news

This way of telling the story is a much more honest and useful approach to conflict. So often in human history, a conflict with "others" is used to deflect attention away from internal group conflicts. We can sweep our own internal difficulties under the rug while we battle "them." This also means that it is in the interests of our leaders to continue external conflict, so that problems inside the group (which usually include problems with our leaders) can be ignored. We can rally around the flag/fatherland/motherland or some other illusion of group cohesion and not talk about how our leaders got us into this mess in the first place.

The Genesis paradigm helps us remember both the failings of our leaders and the larger goal of "being a blessing" that we are supposed to be pursuing. The conflicts with outsiders were quickly and effectively resolved. Using violence and the way of revenge is shown in a negative light (Genesis 34). Yes, we could just try to kill them all, but that hardly makes us better children of God.

So Abraham was called, a promise was made, and he did according to what his calling was. This did not mean the destruction of others. It was about claiming blessing but still learning to do what needed to be done. Just because Abraham was called does not mean that others were not also called. Just because Abraham had a special line to God does not mean that others did not have their own.

Another way to see this is by noticing what is missing from the story. It is always tricky to make an argument from silence, but some silences are louder than others. One of the major silences is the relative lack of direct intervention of God in Abraham's life, at least in comparison with the Exodus story. Abraham traveled from Ur to Haran to Canaan to Egypt and back to Canaan, a distance approaching 1,000 miles. He did all this without manna, quail, pillar of fire, or other obvious signs of God's activity. Yes, God did send visions (15:1) and dreams (20:3), and even showed up in the flesh at one point (Genesis 18), but that hardly compares with plagues and parting bodies of water. There were a few pieces of miraculous intervention but in general nothing that separated Abraham from the people around him. Abraham was not better or different from his neighbors. He treated many people as his equals and occasionally even as his superiors (14:20; 21:27). The story leaves open the possibility that Abraham's was one calling among many.

Another major silence in Genesis is the lack of the word *holiness*. Holiness is about separation. To be holy is to be set apart, to be different from other things. Abraham was not called to be holy. He was not set apart as better than or different from other people. There is a definite sense of order and goodness in Genesis, but no one is exempt from the possibility of being good or evil. Good and evil are about actions, not internal difference.

In Genesis, there is a lot to be said for just getting along. The problem of wickedness is found in big things like killing brothers (Cain and Abel) and can overwhelm the entire earth (the flood), but mostly it is not the major issue. Occasionally it becomes so grievous that destruction is the only option (Sodom and Gomorrah), but mostly God is not worried about who is better than others. Abraham is called, but the calling is not accompanied by a long list of rules or demands from God.

Within this paradigm, security is found in being honest and willing to do what it takes to get along with others, by being right and just (18:19). We are who we are, while allowing others to be others. It is not about separation but about integrity.

This story is, in many ways, like the choices the returning exiles actually made. After their exile in Babylon, they went from Babylon to Jerusalem because they believed they were called to that land by God. This is clear from all their writings. But they did not kill the people they met along the way, neither did they attempt to wipe out the inhabitants of the land once they got there. (They had little choice in this, since the Persians would not have allowed it, but let's give them the benefit of the doubt and presume that they wouldn't have anyway.) In all of this, they had to deal with the Persians and their gods, whether or not they believed these gods were real. They had to get along (to some extent) with the people around them (because Persians did not give them a choice). They had to work hard in the journey and in the land because there was no manna and very little milk and honey. So the stories in Genesis provided a metaphor for their current reality that actually fit their experience.

Genesis also provided a picture of a way forward that did not require miraculous intervention. This does not mean that it denies the existence or activity of God. But it did not require a different God than the one they had experienced on their journey and who they likely experienced once they arrived. It would stand as an assessment of the God-we-have rather than the God-we-want.

In these ways, the book of Genesis provides a significant alternative to the Exodus/Joshua paradigm. It is about cooperation rather than genocide. It provides examples of conflict resolution without warfare. It shows people how to get along with others while still recognizing differences.

Most importantly, it gives us a series of stories that more closely reflect the experiences of the returning exiles and the God who was with them.

DANGERS OF THE GENESIS MODEL

Despite the many and significant ways that Genesis provides a better model for the way forward than does Exodus, it is important not to overstate the ways it can be helpful for us in the 21st century. We cannot simply take these ancient stories and "apply them" directly to any particular current situation. They speak about a world quite different from ours, and there is no going back.

It is also important to deal honestly with the parts of the story that we find troubling. If we are going to be honest about the God-we-have rather than the God-we-want, we need to be willing to be equally honest about the Bible. There are parts of this story that provide negative examples of how to treat people and how to construct a healthy society.

While Genesis portrays Abraham and his family as willing and able to get along with the people who are already living in Canaan, it still portrays the land as ultimately "ours." In this, it looks forward to the Exodus/Joshua model, where the "final solution" will need to be enacted once the "iniquity of the Amorites is ... complete" (15:16). So this attitude of live-and-let-live is portrayed as only temporary, rather than as a long-term response to the existence of others. Even in the midst of these stories of negotiation and give-and-take, we as readers are invited into the fantasy of a land devoid of people who are not "us." This leads further to the fantasy that, if it wasn't for "them," everything would be fine.

Another disturbing part of the Genesis story is that it assumes a strict male hierarchy. This is a core part of its worldview. Women are owned, traded, and used. Slaves are also bought and disposed of. Someone like Hagar, the foreign female slave, suffers from oppression on multiple levels. No one asks Hagar if she wants to have Abram's child (Genesis 16). Abraham is within his rights to allow Sarah to send Hagar off into the wilderness, presumably to die, on two different occasions (Genesis 16, 21). Throughout the text, people exist in situations of clear social stratification, where someone is boss and it probably isn't you. Traditionally most readers identify with Abraham, who does not experience this as an unjust system, but numerically Abraham was just one, with hundreds of people who were beneath him.

You Are Not Going to Heaven (and why it doesn't matter)

In these situations, making peace is the task of leadership. Herdsmen quarrel but are unable to resolve conflict without the intervention of kings and masters (13:7; 21:25). Leaders decide who is friend and who is enemy. You may be required to kill (14:14) or to sleep with your master (16:1–4, 30:3) or the local king (12:15; 20:2) because your husband is afraid of him. If you do want something, even if it is within your rights, you may be required to use trickery to get it (Genesis 38). If you are raped, you may be avenged (whether you want to be or not), but your opinion will not be requested (see Genesis 34). You can be thrown out into the wilderness at any time to fend for yourself, even if you have done nothing wrong (21:8–21).

So clearly this is not a story about people power. There is little in the story that would suggest that peace (or any change) can come from ordinary people acting together. Some people are leaders, and everyone else is to act like sheep. Passivity is not encouraged but is simply assumed. Wives of powerful men have the opportunity to ask (or even demand) certain things (16:2, 5; 21:10) but are not responsible for their own decisions or the consequences of their actions. In general, the lives of everyone are in the hands of a few powerful men, and that is just the way it is.

This is similar to the "good old days" fantasy in parts of America today. Some people want to return to the good old days of the 1950s, when men were men and life was good. What this fantasy wants us to forget is the racism, homophobia, and sexism that grounded the "(white) men were men" theme. Somehow the women who are currently professors in the university where I teach are not excited about a return to this model.

The final danger of the Genesis model is the whole problem of dropping lessons from an ancient context into a modern situation. How do we apply the lessons from conflicts between shepherds to the various complex conflicts we experience today? Obviously adopting a nomadic pastoralist economic system is not an option. For most of us, the solution "just dig another well" must be a metaphor at best. So what do we make it a metaphor for? This does not mean that there is nothing we can learn from these stories. It is just to acknowledge that using these stories will require creativity. We can read for strategies and motivation without needing to copy the solutions.

Old Testament—the good news

STILL

While it isn't possible to go back and rework the mistakes of history, it can be helpful to imagine our history if we had chosen differently. This helps us think about our current situation differently, which further allows us to imagine a new future.

Within the early history of American colonization, as well as the hundreds of parallel stories of European colonialism, the Exodus/Joshua model was part of the religious underpinnings of the project. The language of "promised land" rings throughout American history and with it the attitude toward land and others found in the Exodus/Joshua model.

Now imagine American history under the Genesis model. How would the story be different if "just learn to get along" had been the guiding mantra? Imagine this history with no imperialist ideal, no exceptionalism, and no understanding that, if the land is going to be "ours," then it can't be "theirs."

While changing the past is not an option, the Genesis model can provide another vision for a way forward. How would the foreign policies of most countries change if "just learn to get along" became an expectation from ordinary citizens? What if a declaration of war became a symbol of the failure of our leaders, rather than a symbol of their strength? Again, taking these ancient stories and choosing to be guided by them is not a simple matter of "What Would Abraham Do?", but there are lessons there we have chosen not to explore.

d) Limits and warnings about militarism

PEOPLE WHO READ THE Old Testament often contrast it sharply with the New Testament. They complain about all the bloodshed and violence, especially the war and slaughter either commanded or condoned by God. Others prefer the Old Testament precisely for that reason, using it as a way to explain their own militarism. So this section may come as a surprise to many people. The Old Testament, as we will see, is not as bloodthirsty as it may initially appear. It may not even be as bloodthirsty as we are.

There is some merit to the impression of a war-filled Old Testament, especially when North American society predisposes us to expect a God of unconditional love. When our subconscious vision of God is Santa, the God of the Old Testament comes across as angry, grumpy, and possessing a violent temper. Some of these stories are the kind that many kids love to hear, but we don't really want to tell them.

Yet despite the existence and even centrality of many stories of war, bloodshed and wholesale slaughter, what is equally surprising is the lack of emphasis on militarism. If you asked the average person to name ten people from the Old Testament, it is unlikely that any of them would be a general. There would likely be some kings and/or judges, but these are not commanders of standing armies, and few of them really come across well as military leaders (as we will see). The authority of military leaders and the importance of military hierarchy is carefully limited. Yes, warfare is occasionally necessary, but it is both occasional and when necessary. Victories in battle are celebrated, but they are celebrated at the time of their conclusion, and while they are memorialized in story and song, they are not part of the feasts and festivals of the people. A brief walk through the Old Testament will illustrate what I mean.

Israel's neighbors framed their creation stories as a result of war between the various gods. Obviously this is not an option in the Old Testament, since there is only one God, so the story of the earth must begin in a different context. Warfare is not presented as a normal part of the created order. Instead, harmony is the natural state of things.

Similarly, while many Christians view the world as a battleground between Satan and God, this view is also absent from the Old Testament. Even if we choose to believe that the serpent in Genesis 3 is Satan (a characterization that is not part of the biblical account), the serpent acts through cunning and misdirection rather than through conflict and direct confrontation.

In fact, there are no stories of war in the first thirteen chapters of Genesis. There is certainly conflict, but but large-scale organized killing is not shown as the natural or best way to deal with conflict. Thus, for example, the Tower of Babel story (chapter 11) is devoid of military language, and God's response involves no taking of life. This itself is not surprising, since the last effort to fix things through large-scale killing (Noah, Genesis 6–9) was unsuccessful (see 8:21).

The first war mentioned in Genesis is 14:2 and is presented in a negative way. It is about subjection and the taking of plunder. Abraham's entry into the conflict is described as a rescue mission and he returns with what is his or what belongs to his allies.

Old Testament—the good news

The stories of Moses and the exodus from Egypt could presumably have provided opportunities for the writers to emphasize the fearless heroism and military prowess of the Israelites. Instead, even Moses himself is shown in strikingly nonheroic ways. In response to Egyptian practices of killing Israelite babies, he was hidden in a basket—hardly a propitious beginning for a savior. His entry into salvation-through-warfare, the killing of the Egyptian who beats an Israelite, was only done when he thought no one was looking and he quickly ran away when the deed becomes known (2:11–14). Even when called to a heroic task, he continually attempted to get out of his role, to the point where God got angry (3:1–4:17).

The story of Israel leaving Egypt highlights the power of God, and no mention is made of any military actions on the part of Israel or its leaders. God was a warrior (15:3) but the people weren't. The rest of the story before the entry into Canaan certainly contains its share of bloodshed but has no individual heroes or detailed battle accounts. Neither Moses nor Aaron are portrayed as military heroes. Their task was more concerned with stopping God from destroying the Israelites than leading the people into war.

Inside the law, there are often limits placed on military power. It is important to remember in all this that the law is not set out as "religious" law, but is the whole of the law for the entire people, encompassing all aspects of life. So it would not be surprising to see a section of the law devoted to the formation and maintenance of an army or the creation and duties of the officer or warrior class. Yet these are absent from the law of Israel. Numbers 31 does mention officers from the army, but these do not appear to be permanent positions, and they are mentioned only in relation to Moses' anger with them (31:14). Again, this is not to minimize the horror of the war (including the slaughter of every person except virgin girls, who are taken as plunder) but merely to demonstrate the understanding the text provides of the place of the military in Israelite society.

There are specific rules for battle given in Deuteronomy 20. In the event of war, it is the priest who first addresses the army, encouraging them not to fear and assuring them of God's presence with them (20:3–4). The officers then address the army, outlining the rules for who can go home if they want to (20:5–8), including anyone who is afraid. The text says nothing about from where these officers come, but it is they who then choose a commander for the army (20:9), making it clear that this is also not seen as a permanent position. Again, the assumption appears to be that the army is an occasional force rather than a permanent structure.

Another place we see a significant silence regarding the place of the military is in the laws concerning festivals. Festivals are events traditionally used to commemorate major events in the life of a people, whether natural events (spring, harvest, new moons) or human events. These often include significant victories in battle. Studying the festivals of a people is a good way of understanding who they think they are and what kinds of values they hold.

In the Law, none of the festivals are for victory in battle. They are harvest festivals (Weeks, Tabernacles—see Deuteronomy 16) or the celebration of the Passover. While the Passover certainly is a celebration of liberation, there is no sense in this of "look what we did" or "remember what our army did." The sacrifices decreed at the beginning of Leviticus also have no special ones to request, ensure, or celebrate victory in battle. Sacrifices may have been used in these ways, but this is not part of the descriptions in Leviticus.

The book of Joshua would at first glance appear to break with the de-emphasis on military strength, but even here there are surprises. Despite the overall theme of victory over and utter destruction of the Canaanites, the narrative contains few battle descriptions. There is also no suggestion that battles should be memorialized. The one memorial set up in Joshua is the stones at the edge of the Jordan that celebrate the unopposed entry into the land (Joshua 4:1–7).

So while Joshua himself was clearly a commander of the Israelite army and led them to numerous victories, there is a lack of pomp and ceremony to the story. Joshua is never shown on his war horse riding victoriously into a conquered city. There are no descriptions of his battle armor or his sword. Neither is he described as either particularly fierce or cunning or strong. All credit is given to God. In many places, the text says nothing about what God actually did, but neither does it usually say what the soldiers or the commanders did. The battle scenes are usually brief and lacking in heroic detail.

Likewise, the book of Judges clearly presents a world where war heroes and battles are at the foreground of the story. Yet the presentation of the battles does not highlight the things we might expect in a war story. The battles being fought were not those of imperial expansion but those of liberation, yet even here, it is liberation from the oppressor who has been sent by God because of the sins of the people. So all these battles could presumably have been avoided by basic obedience to the covenant.

Old Testament—the good news

The actual victories seldom go into detail about the strength of the army—in fact, there is no army at all. Judges works with a libertarian ideal, with the army being created at the time of need, rather than being an institution. Even the Judges themselves were military saviors, wimps, and idiots. Gideon was afraid of his own shadow. Samson was entirely dependent on God and used his muscles for brains. Deborah was a woman, and her "general" needed the help of two women (Deborah and Jael) to win the battle.

There is also the larger question of why they are called "judges." This title suggests that their primary duty involved legal decisions, while the stories generally portray them as military leaders. While many reasons have been suggested, one of the effects of this is that their title downplays their role as military leaders. Finally, of course, the whole system falls apart (Judges 19–21), and it becomes clear that this "peace through local warlords" system was not a long-term solution. The people needed stability, and it was not provided by these judges.

Samuel was the last of the judges, and when he got old, the people asked for a king (1 Samuel 8). Neither Samuel nor God were pleased by this, and Samuel warned the people of the drawbacks of monarchy. The first drawback mentioned is the conscription of men for soldiers, as part of an ongoing force rather than for occasional battles. So both God and Samuel agreed that a standing army was a bad idea and represented a decision not to trust God (1 Samuel 8:7). Yet despite God's warnings and Samuel's plots, Saul was declared king. Saul does not appear to do most of the things Samuel and God were concerned about, yet his kingship was still undermined by Samuel, so his rule is more like a blip on the screen, as a transition to David. David then appears as an obvious example of the military hero.

If any figure in the Old Testament is the archetypal military leader, it would be David. He won battles early and often. He defeated the Philistines on numerous occasions and expanded the borders of Israel, extracting tribute from neighboring peoples. So one could use David to present the ideal of a people ruled by military heroes.

But even here, there is a definite downside presented to David and his military emphasis. 2 Samuel is a positive and negative portrayal of king-as-military-hero. It begins in 1 Samuel with the various struggles between Saul and David over who was really king. The war became internal and the lives lost were all Israelites. As 2 Samuel 3:1 says, "There was a long war between the house of Saul and the house of David." This was hardly the purpose of kingship. At one point David even went over to the enemy and lived among the Philistines (1 Samuel 27).

It is also interesting how soon after becoming king David gave over leadership of the military to others. So the focus moves from David-as-military-hero to David-as-just-ruler (2 Samuel 8:15). Joab became the military commander (8:16), and now war was fought because it happened to be spring (11:1). Now David was at home, bored and sleeping with other people's wives (2 Samuel 11), and battles were fought to kill off internal enemies (11: 15–17). Soon the battles again became Israelite vs. Israelite over who was to be king (2 Samuel 18), with the kings being the only winners. Thus, many of these stories could just as easily be used to present the downside of having leaders who use military force as their only problem-solving tool.

The other interesting change in the David stories is the smaller and smaller role given to God. David was initially called and confirmed by God as king, but his wars were not the result of direct orders from God. He did inquire of God before his battle with the Philistines (2 Samuel 5:19), but the initiative was his own. God also promised David rest from his enemies (7:11), but David doesn't appear to be willing to accept that rest, choosing instead to continue to make war. Finally, we have the character of Ahithophel, whose advice was "*as if* one consulted the oracle of God" (16:23), but this just makes one wonder why they didn't actually inquire of God. Whatever we make of David and his glorious victories, we cannot simply assume that the voice of the king in calling for war is the voice of God.

The rest of the kings were not military heroes. Yes, there was an army, but there are few stories of generals or battles. Omri was perhaps the most successful king in terms of expansion through military victory (1 Kings 16:21–28), but we know this only through reconstructing it from other places in the story. He himself receives little recognition for this, since he did not pass the test of following God in the right way.

What we do know of Omri's victories and the success of his royal line is found in the stories of Elijah and Elisha (1 Kings 17—2 Kings 10). Not surprisingly, the focus here is on the prophets and the role of God rather than army size or strategies or brilliant leadership.

One of the most glaring examples of lack of emphasis on military strength is found at the end of the books of Kings. In 2 Kings 17–25, both nations, Israel and Judah, are defeated by foreign armies. The strength or weakness of the Israelite army is not even a factor. Even in victory (2 Kings 19), there is no mention at all of Israel even having an army. Things

Old Testament—the good news

happened according to the will of God and human efforts (even efforts on God's side) were apparently in vain.

The writing prophets are also champions of this perspective. Salvation comes from God and human efforts are insignificant. Most of the times armies are mentioned, it is the armies of Israel's enemies coming to destroy them. This is proclaimed as the will and desire of God, as punishment for Israel's unfaithfulness. Jeremiah 37:10 illustrates this nicely: "Even if you defeated the whole army of Chaldeans who are fighting against you, and there remained of them only wounded men in their tents, they would rise up and burn this city."

This means two things for the prophets. The first is that human military efforts can mean fighting *against* God. If God is fighting on the side of our enemies, then our self-defense is not only useless but an action in opposition to the will of God.

The second and more interesting thing it means is that salvation and defeat are not necessarily opposites. The prophets proclaim that God's salvation could only come through Israel's defeat at the hands of its enemies. Somehow the idea of being saved *by* our enemies through *their* victory does not occur to us regularly. This idea is both counterintuitive and contrary to basic logic. But it is the logic of the prophets.

HISTORICAL SUMMARY

Of course, none of this is particularly surprising in the Persian context. The Israelites who have returned from exile in Babylon do so as part of the Persian empire. So it is unlikely that they would have been allowed to write and proclaim stories of heroics in battle. Any official documents that spoke openly about the glorious Israelite army and its great generals would likely have been considered subversive and would not have survived the 200 years of Persian rule.

So Israel wrote its stories another way. The Passover gave them hope for salvation from foreign oppression, but it was still passive. The people simply must sit and wait for God to act. On their own, they are as likely to fight against God as for God. The same is true for the rest of their story. All this is logical in the Persian period—there is nothing to celebrate and it would be dangerous to celebrate.

For 21st-century readers, the contrast between this way of telling their story and our own is significant. In many parts of the world today, our histories, our public spaces, and our calendars are filled with stories and memorials of war, victories, and important military locations and figures. There are World War I cannons in my local park, despite the fact that the park is thousands of miles from the nearest WWI battle site. In places like this, God may be invoked in various ways, but the assumption always is that human armies are essential. It is also assumed that God is always fighting on our side. Neither of these perspectives is shared by the Old Testament.

Often the Bible is used when describing how these victories are attributable to God or how God was active in the battle. Yet the character and the tone of these memorials is quite different from the stories of battles we have seen in the Old Testament. These memorials set a tone and expectation for the future and affect our attitudes toward conflict resolution and dealing with our neighbors. Trust in God has been replaced by trust in military strength, although these are often passed off as the same thing. Biblically, however, they are opposites.

The most obvious example from the Bible is the destruction of Jerusalem by the Babylonian army, the event that led to the exile. 2 Kings 24:2, 3 states that the Babylonians and others were sent by God to destroy Judah. The prophet Jeremiah utters similar judgments repeatedly. To fight against the Babylonian invaders is to fight against God. If Judah had an army large enough to defend itself, it would still have been insufficient because God was clearly on the other side.

This type of language is consistently absent from any modern military memorials, even in cases like Vietnam, when "our" troops were not victorious. It is difficult to even imagine a section of the Vietnam Veterans Memorial dedicated to explaining why God fought against America in that war. This idea, so important to the biblical notion of salvation, is anathema to the modern discussion. We may put "In God We Trust" on our coins, but we do not trust God to choose on whose side to fight.

THE DANGERS OF THESE LIMITS

We have seen the stark contrast between the biblical images of military strength and those of most 21st-century nations. This is true even, and maybe especially, in places that lay claim to a Christian or Jewish heritage. The question, though, is what replaces these images.

In the Persian period, the people of Israel had no army of their own. They likely had some military presence, but these soldiers would have been under Persian control and were as likely to be used against the Jews as for them. The implication in their stories appears to be that, if we have no army, there is nothing we can do. The options generally highlighted are either large-scale violence or complete passivity. The only hope for change is direct intervention from God, so we can merely sit and wait.

I find this same attitude prevalent in my classroom all the time. Either kill or do nothing. This attitude, however, is not the way my students live their lives. They are constantly negotiating, striving, and seeking justice, opportunities, and freedom in nonviolent ways. They have been taught these skills all their lives. Yet somehow when it comes to large-scale problem-solving, they resort to an all-or-nothing solution. They must have learned this somewhere, and I fear that the Bible is part of the problem. If the Bible tells them it's the army or nothing, and their entire worldview tells them that *nothing* is not an option, then the army must be the answer. Or if they read in the Bible that God will save them from their enemies, and their history claims that God works through their military (although not anyone else's), why should they doubt? Surely the victories of our armies are proof enough (and we don't talk about the defeats). In these and other ways, the Bible becomes a significant part of a worldview where a strong military is "our" only hope for freedom and security. They are fed these buzz-words so often that they are just "true."

STILL

The Old Testament is often refreshingly honest about the world we live in. It is not a pacifist panacea but an interesting combination of hard-nosed realism and bountiful hope. Yet even in this hope, it is not wildly optimistic about the chances that human violence will bring about lasting peace. There is never the sense that just one more war will return us to Eden. There is no belief in a war to end all war.

It also shows us that a community can exist without being obsessed with its military strength. The people of Israel were well aware of the bloodshed and violence in their own history but chose not to project this infinitely into the future. They never claimed that the blood of soldiers brought them closer to God. They never talked about death in war as a sacrifice. War, according to the Old Testament, does not make you holy. If you die, you are dead. A few may be remembered, but for the most part your only hope for being remembered is through the life you have left behind, through your children and grandchildren. And even in death, people are remembered for much more than their willingness to kill.

Christians today are often put off by the violence in the Old Testament. There is reason for this, but on the whole the Old Testament is not as violent as most "Christian" nations have been and are. There are few people today who would be willing to follow the ancient Israelites in preferring not to have a standing army. There are few who are willing to proclaim that God is actively fighting against them. Even people not willing to take up Jesus' challenge to love their enemies will generally find many other challenges in the Old Testament, should they be willing to look past the surface.

e) Wisdom

THUS FAR, WE HAVE seen that salvation, the central message of the church, is linked to a community process that begins with a basic contentment, getting along with others, and limits on the glory we heap on our military prowess. This section will add another piece of the puzzle but will focus more on the *how* of salvation than the *what*.

In adding *wisdom* to our picture, we get an understanding of a salvation that comes from a long, slow process of becoming rather than from the latest and greatest. It will not happen today or tomorrow, so we need to stop and think and plan. We need to ask questions—What have we learned? How does this guide us? What didn't work (things not to try again)? What might we do better next time? Salvation arises from doing what works and not doing what doesn't. In this, we also need to figure out which goals are worthwhile. The energy and excitement of youth needs to be supplemented and complemented by the long-term vision and experience of those who have been around a while. This is another part of "we are all in this together."

PURSUING WISDOM

In the Old Testament, wisdom is a goal in itself. It is worth pursuing for its own sake. We first see this goal in Genesis 3:6, where the fruit (you may know it as an apple) was desired "to make one wise." In this case, wisdom is equated with "be(ing) like God, knowing good and evil" (3:5). So wisdom

Old Testament—the good news

is not a small thing in the Bible. To be wise is to be like God. This is not surprising for, as we will see, wisdom comes from God.

Of course, pursuing wisdom for its own sake should also have benefits for the larger community. For example, in Deuteronomy 1:13–15, leaders were chosen on the basis of wisdom. In this passage, wisdom is paired with "discerning and reputable." This gives us more insight into what wisdom actually is. Wisdom is about making good choices. It involves understanding the situation as it exists, figuring out which path is best for the future (discerning), and about doing this consistently (reputable). This also shows us the link between wisdom and age. Wisdom is acquired through experience and is demonstrated over time. This does not mean, of course, that experience and age always lead to wisdom. Some people manage to make the same mistakes over and over again. The biblical writers were well aware of this, which is why reputation was important. One of the questions the Bible continues to ask is how to know wisdom when you see it.

An aspect of biblical wisdom that is still an issue today is the relationship between wisdom and gender. The Hebrew word "wisdom" is a feminine noun, which may or may not have had any impact on the way people thought about wisdom. Obviously this has little influence on the English translations, except where "Wisdom" becomes a female figure in Proverbs (more below).

2 Samuel 14 is the story of a wise woman from Tekoa, who is brought into the story specifically by Joab, commander of David's army, in order to guide David toward a particular course of action. The narrative is detailed, and shows the woman using skills in order to make this happen, including allegory and flattery. In this instance, her wisdom did not come in the form of specific advice to the king but in the ways she spoke to him to bring him to make a particular decision. So the king believed that he had chosen on the basis of his own wisdom, which the woman characterized as "like the wisdom of the angel of God to know all things that are on the earth" (14:20), but really he had been conned into this course of action by someone who truly had wisdom.

Another story about a wise woman is in 2 Samuel 20. There Joab was besieging a city in order to capture a particular person in the city. A wise woman from the city spoke with Joab, found out what he wanted, and convinced the people of the city to kill the man in order to save the city. This woman also used words skillfully to find out what must be done to end the siege (see verses 18, 19) and presumably also to makes the plan come about.

There is also the implication in the story that her status as "wise woman" was what convinced Joab to listen to her, even as his soldiers were battering down the city walls.

These stories show clearly that wisdom is not limited to men. Women of wisdom become people of influence, even in a society that is strongly inclined to male leadership. The salvation of the city is not found in the strength of armies or the number of weapons or the wisdom of its male leadership. In fact, it is the stereotypically male form of wisdom ("If all else fails, you need a bigger hammer.") that is shown to be pointlessly violent in these stories, and it required the intervention of women to point this out. So wisdom is found where wisdom is found, which then also becomes true of salvation.

These two stories, taken together, also suggest a connection between wisdom and rhetoric. Wisdom is not just knowing what is right but being able to guide people toward a particular set of actions. A person may acquire a reputation as a "wise person," but that only gets them into the discussion. At that point, they can't simply rely on their reputation but must be able to employ the skills they have acquired toward a particular end. This understanding of wisdom makes it an active skill set that involves more than simply sitting on a chair and dispensing good advice.

Obviously King Solomon is the central figure in the Bible when it comes to wisdom. Besides the stories about him in 1 Kings, there are the psalms (72, 127), the book of Ecclesiastes, and most of the book of Proverbs (see 1:1 and 30:1). Solomon's wisdom is highlighted in 1 Kings when he initially asked for "an understanding mind to govern your people, able to discern between good and evil" (3:9), after God offered him anything he wanted. God added wisdom to the gift (3:12) as well as other things.

The stories told of Solomon's wisdom include the ruling given to the two women concerning the baby (3:16–28), which concludes by noting that the people saw that "the wisdom of God was in him, to execute justice." In addition there is a section specifically extolling Solomon's wisdom (4:29–34), which adds that Solomon also spoke of the natural sciences, suggesting that wisdom is not limited to an understanding of the human world.

The stories noting Solomon's wisdom conclude with the visit of the Queen of Sheba (1 Kings 10:1–13). This story links the wisdom of Solomon with his increasing wealth. He answered all the questions the Queen had for him, and she gave him gifts. Her statements are also interesting in that she linked Solomon's wisdom with the happiness of his household (verse 8) and also noted that the purpose of this wisdom was to "execute justice and righteousness" (verse 10).

Of course, all of this falls apart in 1 Kings 11, when his heart turned away from God. This is blamed on his foreign wives (11:4), as if wise Solomon wasn't responsible for his own decision. It is difficult to know whether this part of the story affects our understanding of the value of wisdom. Perhaps we can take this as a warning against the hazard that women pose to the male intellect (or not). Or perhaps it is a warning to men about the importance of thinking with our heads rather than with other parts of our body.

While neither of Solomon's psalms use the word "wisdom," there are other Psalms that are often classified as "wisdom Psalms." These include Psalms 36, 37, 49, 73, 78, 112, 127, 128, 133, although a discussion of wisdom is not limited to these Psalms. These are not so much *about* wisdom but are collections of sayings like we would expect to find in Proverbs.

The book of Proverbs itself begins with a section dedicated to convincing the reader that the pursuit of wisdom is worthwhile (chapters 1–9). It details the benefits of wisdom and the folly of its opposite. In this section, the figure of Wisdom is played by a young woman, while her opposite is played by another woman who is adulterous (again, those crafty women!).

This suggests that, even in ancient societies, the pursuit of wisdom was not a self-evident goal. People desired all sorts of things. Proverbs seems to be specifically written to wealthy young men, people who had the time to be contemplating all sorts of wild things and had the means to carry out their plans. To counter this, Proverbs offers the alternative of long-term satisfaction and health. The "lips of a loose woman drip honey," but that way leads to death (Proverbs 5:4, 5). Long life and prosperity are the rewards of wisdom.

This is also a significant piece of wisdom for our time. In a world dominated by short-term gain and quick fixes, the church offers an ancient book full of difficult writings, combined with often quaint traditions and old-fashioned ideas. This is hardly a recipe for success. That is, unless you define success in terms of the long-term health and even the survival of human society. Somehow we have managed to produce many versions of the iPhone without significant progress toward any goal besides the enrichment of Apple shareholders. Will the next incarnation of the iPhone finally result in an end to child poverty or human trafficking?

Obviously change will continue to be the only constant. This will include changes in the church and in our understanding of the Bible. Without wisdom, however, change is just "new stuff." Some old problems will be fixed, other problems will be created, and our society will continue rudderless and largely pointless. The illusion of liberal vs. conservative will dominate the political landscape, as some people argue for some grand new vision for the future, while others argue for a return to some illusory version of the past. Neither of these represents wisdom, and neither will lead to salvation.

THE DANGERS OF WISDOM

The dangers of the promotion of wisdom are well-known to the biblical writers. In fact, the Old Testament may contain more about the problems of wisdom than its benefits. In the background is a whole series of discussions about the causes of Israel's problems, the roles of various people in the past, present, and future of Israel and the general shape that this future should take. In many ways, this discussion was at the heart of Jewish identity as it existed in a world controlled by foreign empires.

This may seem significantly irrelevant to you. After all, many people reading this book will live in democratic countries where the government, and therefore presumably the present and future, are controlled by the people. This would make the discussion of how to live in a world not under your own control simply hypothetical. I would suggest, however, that you take a moment to think about exactly how much influence you, your social network, and your community have in the larger political world. In many ways, we are all living in a world where many decisions about our lives are being made by others. So learning from the discussions of others can be helpful in negotiating the line between owning the power we have and recognizing the power others have over us.

This discussion is also increasingly relevant for the church. We are living in a post-Christian world. Governments around the world no longer need to ask the church's permission to act. They no longer seek the advice of church leadership on matters of state or policy. The church can make statements on all sorts of issues, and they will be ignored by politicians of all parties.

Another danger of wisdom is that too much emphasis on tradition can lead to stagnation. The revolutionary movement soon becomes the revolutionary party which soon becomes the gathering of the elderly remembering the good old days and moaning how the movement has all gone downhill since they were young. The movement itself easily becomes a matter of saying the right catch phrases and singing the old songs. In this scenario, the "wisdom" of the elders is filled with ideas and strategies that are responses to the problems of a different generation.

A similar kind of thing happens when wisdom becomes stuck, and the group, now an institution, continues to do the same thing again and again while expecting different results. So the church, in many places a dying institution, holds an old-fashioned tent revival because that was such an effective tool for renewal and growth in the old days.

Another problem with wisdom, which we see operating in the background in the Bible, is that it usually works better for the rich than for the poor. The system as it exists works well for the rich. After all, it made them rich, and besides, they are the ones who make the rules. So "we" need to keep following in the same path, for any other path threatens the status quo.

This is shown in both Proverbs and Ecclesiastes. Proverbs is a handbook of values for wealthy young men. For them, the prevailing wisdom is to settle down, mind your elders, and don't do anything to endanger your inherited position in society. It is the young person of means who is tempted because he has the leisure time and funds to get into trouble. Conversely, he is also the one with the most to lose by not following traditional wisdom.

The same can be said for the writer of Ecclesiastes. He is someone who has the time and money to explore and contemplate, and the time and money to ponder and write. The poor are often too busy surviving or serving the rich to have those options. You only get to choose if you have a choice. Choosing between work and starvation is not a real choice.

Ecclesiastes also has much to say directly about the limits of wisdom. The writer claims to have sought and acquired wisdom but ultimately declares, "For in much wisdom is much vexation, and those who increase knowledge increase sorrow" (1:18). So while wisdom is much to be preferred over foolishness (2:13), it is still vanity (2:19).

The book of Job is equally sarcastic about the usefulness of wisdom. Job's "wise" friends gathered to give him advice, but their answers were consistently wrong, as God says in 42:8. They were even mocked by one of their own in the speeches of Elihu in chapters 32—37. Then God continued to mock the wisdom and understanding of humans in general in his reply to Job (chapters 38–41), and Job was left to "repent in dust and ashes" (42:6).

Yet the wisdom of the friends is portrayed as worse, and they were required to sacrifice as a sign of their repentance (42:7–9).

The prophets are also not impressed with wisdom. Isaiah continues to mock the wise in various places. He talks about those who are "wise in your own eyes" (5:21), and calls the wise counselors of Pharaoh "stupid" (19:11). He foretells the end of the "wisdom of the wise" (29:14) because God makes their knowledge foolish (44:25). Jeremiah is equally unimpressed with the wisdom of the leaders of Israel (8:8, 9).

This, of course, is hardly surprising coming from the prophets. It is likely they were regularly in competition with the "wise men" of the court for the ear of the king and the people. Does the word of God come through wisdom or through the prophets? Is there a new word from God, or is tradition our best guide to God's will? Both sides marshaled their arguments and presented their cases. It is likely that the main reason we have the writings of the prophets available to us is that they regularly turned out to be right.

In this scenario, wisdom is the voice that suggests caution and urges a steady-as-we-go approach to things. Change is unnecessary or must be undertaken carefully and slowly. The prophets show us that, in the face of impending disaster, continuing to do what we always have done may not be the best course. Sometimes a radical new idea must break in. For the prophets, the armies of Assyria or Babylon were at the gates. We may or may not be at that point yet, but in any case, continuing on our current path is not always the best answer.

STILL

Looking at both the strengths and limits of wisdom, it is not difficult to imagine a balance. There is a place for wisdom and a place for something new to break in. But we also need to admit that this balance is not evident today. Tradition is out; new and improved is in.

The church is caught in this as well, but here we have a problem. Many churches are looking for new ways to do almost everything, yet we are still stuck with this 2,000-year-old book. No matter how young and hip the cover and the presentation, the words and the worldview are ancient.

So we can continue to find ways to make the Bible seem new-and-improved, producing interactive hypertexts with manga graphics or Barbie action figures (and we will). We could also, whether in addition to or as alternative to the postmodern Bible, learn to revere our tradition as tradition.

Old Testament—the good news

There is still a place for the wisdom of the ages, the wisdom of God, as it can be applied to our current reality. The church could become a place where we slow down and look forward by looking back. It could be the one space in our week where we stop running around like hyperactive toddlers, and sit and listen to elders. It could also be that rare time when old and young get together to actually talk to one another and try to understand each other.

Another space for wisdom in our world and in the church opens when we remember that wisdom is not about a set of answers but is a process. We are faced with myriad choices and decisions inside and outside the church, some of which lead toward salvation, while others don't. If we need to choose anyway, why not choose wisely? Learning about wisdom and practicing wisdom can become part of any discussion or discernment.

A recognition of the value and practice of wisdom can also serve as an important alternative to the idea that science will solve all our problems. In this instance, wisdom is that voice that reminds us that science will also create a new set of problems for us and that science, for all its benefits, has already created many of the problems we are facing.

This is not to suggest that wisdom provides an easy answer. Throughout this book I have been continuing to press home the idea that God may also not solve all our problems, and historically seems disinclined to fix what we break. Merely replacing "God" with "science," however, is no more realistic a solution. This is especially important when science is not coupled with ethics. If we do things just because we can, we regularly learn that self-destruction is also something we can do.

In all this, it is also important not to create too strong a link between wisdom and tradition. We see this in the near-death of the church in Europe. Looking at it from the outside, it appears that the church in Europe has decided to maintain tradition at all costs. Now we see the cost and doubt that this was the path of wisdom.

On the other hand, the church in North America is thriving in ever-changing forms. So the traditional brick-and-mortar church has been supplemented by storefront churches, house churches, big-box churches, Internet churches, and a whole range of other forms. However, this does not solve the question of wisdom. Is it really wise to make the church a second-rate copy of the rest of society?

Wisdom does not provide us with a ready-made answer, and we should recognize that "yes" may be the correct one. After all, the "traditional" church was also modeled on the social and architectural realities of its day. But even as we copy the Walmart sales model because it is effective, we need the wisdom to ask Effective for what end? Church growth is not the same as salvation.

This emphasis on wisdom should also not be understood as a new form of generation gap. The Bible is clear that there is no necessary connection between age and wisdom. So just as age does not always bring wisdom, so youth does not preclude it. This is evident in the numbers of young people and students who are reading the church fathers and other masters of wisdom. Books written centuries ago by the wise women and men of their day continue to be read by many. So while many youth (and older people who should know better) may be running after the hottest new style or fastest new gizmo, others are seeking wisdom. They are also doing both at the same time, reading Julian of Norwich on their iPads and learning meditation through websites.

An additional use for wisdom is to understand it as a paradigm for reading the Bible. Too often the Bible becomes a book of rules. So Bible study is a matter of learning the rules and then trying to figure out how to apply them in a radically different world. Or the Bible becomes a holy object, so that having one on the shelf is a necessity, but reading it is optional. Or the Bible must be "modernized" so that its words are directly applicable to life today.

Alternatively, the Bible can be understood as ancient wisdom, a path to the mind of God, and a set of guide markers, so that today's answers can be influenced by something that has stood the test of time. In this sense, the age of the Bible becomes a positive feature. It doesn't sound like everything else. It doesn't fit easily or neatly into our societies. It isn't always easy to understand. It is those features that allow it to speak a new word to us, that is also an ancient word. Then we start Bible study with the recognition that this won't be easy and may not be fun. If you want easy and fun, just watch the screen and turn your brain off. If you want wisdom, that comes in other forms.

Finally, wisdom as a paradigm may also provide a way to engage other faiths. As we encounter the texts and traditions of others as forms of wisdom, we are not locked into simple accept-or-reject options. These can be understood as forms of wisdom, as ways that the wisdom of God has entered our world. This is not the same as saying all religions are the same. It is to say that part of the way forward for our world must include mutual respect. Whatever the future for our planet, our ability to kill each other will only increase, so the opposite pull of cooperation and mutual admiration must also become stronger.

f) Recognizing the whole range of human emotions

ONE OF THE KEYS to salvation is honesty. This is true no matter how we define salvation. Part of this honesty is emotional honesty, admitting to and dealing with the emotions we really feel rather than just the ones we are supposed to feel. Fortunately the Bible can be helpful in this regard, as it often deals with emotions that we would rather pretend we don't have.

Now in general, the Bible is not a particularly emotional book. Individual emotions are usually not recorded; other things take precedence. For example, when Adam and Eve are driven out of the Garden of Eden by God (Genesis 3:24), nothing is said about how they feel. The next verse simply records them as having sex and babies, also apparently without emotion.

This lack of emotional clues is one of the features of the Bible that makes it difficult for modern readers. They want to get a glimpse into the inner lives of the characters, and these are not provided. This also means that, when we do find emotions recorded, we need to pay attention.

Emotions are expressed most often through poetry. Something big happens, so someone composes a poem/prayer. This reflects the dramatic nature of the text. It is difficult to imagine people running around spontaneously breaking into poems. Neither is it likely that women who conceived spontaneously started creating psalms of praise. But the Bible inserts these bits in important places, recording emotion in a specific form.

In understanding how this makes sense, it is important to remember that the Bible was written as an aid to oral performance. Since roughly 95 percent of the people in the ancient world were illiterate, the only experience most people had of the Bible was having it read to them. These readings would have been significant events, so logically they would have been done well. After all, this text was important, so mumbling and stumbling through a reading would have been disrespectful, not to mention pointless. This text was supposed to serve as a major foundation for life, and this importance would have been dramatized in its reading.

If we understand the text as a dramatic presentation, it is not surprising to see poems in especially emotional spots in the text. Poems are ways of attempting to communicate something beyond words, and emotions are certainly beyond simple description. So rather than simply recording the emotions of the event (e.g. "Hannah was very happy..."), the text of 1 Samuel 2 records the various emotions involved so that they can be conveyed both in form and in words ("My heart exults in the LORD; my strength is exalted in my God. My mouth derides my enemies, because I rejoice in my victory," 2 Samuel 2:1).

The Bible presents the various emotions of the human story. Of course, this regularly includes the many positive ones—love, joy, peace, etc. These are the comfortable ones, the ones we expect from the Bible. These are the emotions that are acceptable in church and that we can express on a Sunday morning. In many places, this is the full range of allowable emotions. Not only are our lives supposed to be filled with sweetness and light throughout the week, but we are told to feel positive emotions in negative situations. Funerals become occasions to rejoice that someone is in heaven. Loss of a job means that God is going to bring us new and wonderful opportunities. Difficulties in our families (if we admit these at all) are occasions to learn patience. And God is just sitting in heaven waiting to pour blessings on anyone who asks (apparently Jesus just didn't ask often enough).

This approach to faith means the believer needs to encounter a severely edited version of the Bible. Luckily this is already available to us in the lectionary. The lectionary regularly edits passages to exclude pieces with uncomfortable emotions, especially in the Psalms. Churches that don't use the lectionary have to do this on their own, but the Bible is certainly large enough for the pastor to choose acceptable pieces to read and preach on. And lay people who read the Bible on their own have access to many study guides that often steer them away from things they don't want to think about or that give them ways to believe the text really isn't saying what it appears to be saying.

These are all ways of showing us the Bible-we-want rather than the Bible-we-have. This is a necessary complement to the God-we-want. After all, if the Word of God shows us a different God from the one we worship, what are we going to do? The Bible-we-have, however, also contains many instances of the other emotions, those we aren't supposed to feel. These emotions are also not limited to evil humans or even humans in general. God is often described as feeling anger, hatred, wrath, and the desire for revenge.

In theory, this should give us ways of incorporating the whole range of human emotions in our spiritual experiences. If God feels anger, then our own anger does not separate us from God. If the Bible has a significant place for fear in the life of the believer, then there is no reason for us to pretend we don't feel fear. This allows us to come as whole people before God

Old Testament—the good news

and be whole people with one another. Honesty with the Bible can lead to honesty with our neighbors because honesty is habit forming, and honesty is usually the best place to start. If we cannot be honest with the Bible and with God, if we stand before God pretending to feel something we don't, it is difficult to imagine how we are going to be of value to the world.

REAL BIBLICAL EMOTIONS

This section assumes that you know the nice emotions. I realize that there is still much to be learned from a solid study of the biblical concept of love and joy and other positive emotions. I also know that if you want to study these, there are many guides available already. The list below is meant to be an additional resource, allowing you to complete the picture.

fear

We begin here because fear is such a significant emotion in the Bible. Keep in mind that the people of Israel, both before, during, and after the exile, had many good reasons to fear. There were the basic fears that confront any human being—fear of loss, pain, and tragedy. Then there were fears specific to subsistence farming—drought, plagues, death in childbirth, death of children from a host of diseases or accidents, wild animals, and bandits. Then there were fears specific to people always living between great empires that cared nothing for their lives—whether it was the Egyptians, Arameans, Babylonians, Persians, or more local enemies. There was also the fear of death, especially because the idea of a positive afterlife is largely absent from the Old Testament.

The Bible, on the other hand, proclaims that there is really only one thing to fear—God. So it continues to say that the fear of God is the beginning of wisdom. Now many people have suggested that this word "fear" really means respect. While this has some merit, it is important to remember that, according to the Bible, God does things. And sometimes God does bad things. All things, after all, come from the hand of God.

This means that God is the only thing worthy of fear. The fear of enemies should be replaced by fear of God (Numbers 14:9). After all, if God is truly in control, what else is there to be afraid of?

This is a very difficult idea to bring forward into a postmodern worldview. It is hard to imagine a youth group today where they genuinely are scared of God. It is hard to imagine youth leaders or parents who want this for their kids, or who feel this way themselves. The God of unconditional love has largely overwhelmed any other biblical portrayal of God in our time (think God as Barney the dinosaur).

On the other hand, it is not like fear has been banished from our lives. America spends more on weapons of war than the rest of the world combined, so it must be afraid of something. When you add to this the level of incarceration in so many nations, the general political atmosphere, and the advertising industry that thrives on people being fearful of being out of fashion or behind on technology, it is clear that fear is a major driving force in the world today. To list all the fears that drive us and then declare all these things unworthy of fear would be a major step. Even if we could not suggest the fear of God as an alternative, we could offer the love of God as another way of perceiving the world.

At the very least, it is important that the church not simply add another thing to our list of fears. If the idea of fearing God is simply added on to all the other fears that control our lives, then the church is simply mimicking the fear-based society around us. People are pushed to live their lives on the basis of fear, and the church takes advantage of this instead of offering an alternative.

anger

Anger and wrath are significant emotions in the Bible. They are also the emotions most attributed to God. While God can never be said to fear, God certainly gets angry. God gets angry at individuals and at groups. God gets angry at Israel and at Israel's enemies. Sometimes God even gets angry at people who are doing their best (2 Samuel 6:6, 7).

Much of this, of course, follows from the idea that God is responsible for everything. These passages are not descriptions of the actual emotions of God. Emotions, as we experience them, are biochemical events. It is generally assumed that God is not subject to biochemical changes, since God is not a physical being. So God does not "feel" anger like we do. But somehow we must speak about God and make sense of the world around us, so the language of strong emotion is used to provide a helpful parallel between God's view of things and our own.

For our purposes, it is enough to note that anger is a regular part of the way the Bible thinks about both divine and human actions. Anger happens as a normal part of life. This is, of course, not news to anyone who works with people on a regular basis. People get angry, some more than others, and anger often leads to destruction.

The point is simply that the Bible, when approached honestly, is far from a book about sweetness and light. It is about real things and attempts to help us encounter both the highs and lows of life. We get angry. Let's start there and see where it leads us rather than pretending we don't or shouldn't.

hatred

Hatred, like anger, is a regular part of the Bible. The word is used more than forty times in the Psalms alone. God hates evildoers (Psalm 5:5). Some people hate me, and God rescues me from them (9:13), or I destroyed them (18:40). I hate the company of evildoers (26:5). Hatred is more difficult to deal with because it is one of the opposites of love. You can love someone and be angry with them at the same time. Love and hatred do not fit together as easily.

Again, the simple temptation is to pretend that we don't hate. It is certainly not an emotion that needs to be encouraged. It is, however, a matter of honesty. There is evil in the world, and God is not impressed (Psalm 45:7). Sometimes, when things are going really badly, it feels like God hates us (Deuteronomy 1:27). Some people may hate us. Some people hate God. Others appear to hate justice or peace. There are things we hate, whether rightly or wrongly. And we can cover all this with pink frosting and pretend it isn't there, or we can deal with it. Dealing with the hatred we find in the Bible should also give us an opportunity to deal with our own hatred and talk about people who hate us.

and more

Besides those listed above, the Bible is also willing to talk about the desire for revenge, sadness, despair, anxiety, hopelessness, and other emotions the church too often tries to avoid. These are all part of being human and living in a very imperfect world. In response to these, we could attempt to fill our lives and our churches with spiritual kitsch and feed on a steady diet of chicken soup and chocolate, or we could be honest about who we are and what we feel.

I am not suggesting that we should not accentuate the positive and focus on the love of God. There is enough fear in the world without needing to create more of it. But we experience negative emotions inside ourselves and from others. Either we find a way to incorporate them into our faith or we create an artificial, often irrelevant faith. The God-we-want can easily become cute and furry, which also makes God seem powerless in the face of real evil.

THE DANGERS OF DOING EMOTIONS BADLY

When doing it thoughtfully and consistently, the church can use the Bible as a way to open itself to a wider range of human emotions. This, then, allows it to speak more honestly about life, about the problems we all face as citizens of the world, and about how we solve problems. The difficulties that arise mostly come from not doing this well.

The first potential pitfall is that too often the church already puts too much emphasis on emotions. This is in many ways simply a reflection of our culture. After almost any sporting event, the first question asked of an athlete is some version of, How do you feel? So the church highlights the positive emotions of salvation or worship and attributes negative emotions to a lack of correct religious experience or insight. Now we add an additional emotional layer on to this, and all faith becomes an emotional roller coaster. Intellectual discussion is lost because it doesn't make us feel good. Service is judged by its emotional impact on the one doing the serving ("I felt so blessed.") or the other being served ("They were so happy."). Now add negative emotions into the discussion, and there is nothing else worth talking about. Adding "feel bad" to the more usual "feel good" religious experience is not a significant step forward.

A second pitfall in focusing on negative emotions is that it can lead to acting on them. This is especially problematic when we note that God also feels these emotions and acts on them. So God was angry at some people and punished them. Does this mean that when I get angry at people and strike out at them my actions are Godlike? This has been a temptation throughout church history, where the church has often seen itself as the agent of God's wrath (and often on both sides of a battle). It continues to be true today, where pastors and priests and chaplains willingly send people (and go themselves) to visit God's wrath on an enemy of the state. It becomes especially troubling when the church aligns itself with a particular state or political party and becomes an agent of fear and mistrust.

STILL

Despite these potential dangers, honesty about the emotions we actually feel is better than pretending that we only feel good things. Denial is not a helpful tool in fashioning a positive future for ourselves or our planet. This is especially true when we claim that an angry or hateful response is really an act of love. This is often the case in revenge, where we want to pretend that our actions are motivated by more altruistic thoughts than by the emotions we really feel. Sometimes, too, acting out of anger or hatred is the most loving thing we are capable of doing at the time. In these situations, we hope others will intervene and stop us from acting. They will do this if they are honest about the emotions they see in us.

Using the Bible to acknowledge the emotions we are really feeling also means that these emotions can be discussed inside the church. This is much to be preferred over sanitized church services, which are either devoid of emotion or only sweetness and light. Whatever it is the church means when it offers people salvation, it is not salvation from certain kinds of emotions. We still feel some of these emotions occasionally, and reading about these emotions in the Bible should give us space to confess and be forgiven. This form of honesty takes pressure off the need to always appear happy and successful. It also involves salvation from the need to pretend that we are something we are not.

g) God

For postmoderns, "God" is the perfect sign. "God" is both Something and no-thing, a word about things (?) beyond words. It is a symbol whose referent does not "exist" the way other referents do. "God" is the excess of language, the language of experience beyond language.

The "biblical" God is no less complicated. Sometimes loving Father and sometimes abusive husband, usually male but logically beyond sex if not gender, alternately slow to anger and quick to wrath, absent yet present, silent yet speaking (when not speaking through silence): the enigma wrapped in a puzzle.

Given all this, it is little wonder that atheism is an appealing (and logical) alternative for many people. If God is beyond description, then logically we really don't *know* what we are talking about when speaking of

God. And if we don't know what we are talking about, why are we having this conversation? How can we use words like "real" and "true" when also claiming to be beyond language?

The situation becomes even more complicated when we realize that Western society is functionally polytheistic (believing in more than one god). That is, most North American and European people simply assume that there can only be one God. So when polls are taken about religious belief, the question is asked about whether people believe in God, but never the question "Which one?" Yet most people worship many things or ideas, creating a whole pantheon of gods in their lives.

This is easily seen if we think about faith in God. If we understand faith as trust and loyalty (an idea largely assumed in the Bible), we quickly discover that people are loyal to many things. When we look for signs of worship, the same thing applies. Even modern architecture testifies to the existence of many gods in our society, when tracked by the size and prominence of the various "temples" to the gods of money, sports, and power. The 9/11 bombers understood fully what Americans functionally worship and targeted major temples. They deliberately chose temples to the gods of money, military power, and political power. No churches were targeted, but centers of worship were key. So while we claim to "believe in" one God, we worship many things and proclaim ultimate loyalty to ideas, causes, and pieces of cloth ("I pledge allegiance to . . .").

The church needs to be very careful when proclaiming a unique connection to God. Gods surround us on every side. We are surrounded by religious fanatics ("Rock Chalk," proclaim the faithful around me, while others worship the gods of war, nationalism, or money). Is the church really adding something when it proclaims its faith in God, or is this just another way that the church mimics the rest of society?

The Bible understands this reality fully. Every part of the Bible was written by people who were surrounded by polytheistic cultures. For much of its history, Israel was also a polytheistic society, no matter how much the Bible tries to paper this over. So the proclamation of one God is more a claim to know God better. It is also a claim that some ideas about God are more true than others. Perhaps a story will help make sense of this thought.

A bomber flies over a town. The plane has avoided the various weapons that have attempted to stop it on its mission and drops its load, raining destruction on the town below. The crew may go on to proclaim the experience of God protecting them on their mission. The survivors below may

Old Testament—the good news

experience God when they are spared. They also may experience God as they grieve the dead. Those who are injured may experience God, who is with them in their suffering and recovery. Some may curse God who has not protected the town. Some may decide that the entire incident is a clear indication that there is no God. Each side in the conflict may assume that God is on their side. Various observers may later proclaim certain (or all) these experiences as acts of God or as "not God," for a wide variety of reasons.

In the Bible, we can find validation for all of this language about "God." God is portrayed both as the one who protects soldiers during conquest and the one who saves from enemies who attack. God is both the one who does and the one who does not rescue people in times of distress. God is the one who does or does not bring healing. Jesus and Paul both spent considerable time in conflict with people who worship the same god, which suggests that the god question was still open for debate in their time (and ours).

Even atheists find validation in the Bible. What is the cross, after all, besides the death of God (literally?) and certainly the death of the idea that God will rescue us from all our troubles? God is everything and no-thing, somewhere between the foundation of all being and a mere sign that ultimately denies the reality of the world around us.

Theologically, the word used to describe this mess is "ineffable," meaning that God is beyond knowing. Is it cheating to call God ineffable? If we admit that, finally, we don't really know what we're talking about, it is unlikely to inspire confidence. Or is this simply the path to honesty?

It is important for you to know that I write this section prayerfully, "knowing" beyond any doubt that Something/Someone is "out there," beyond the edges of language. I know both things: that God is, and that God "is" not, at least not the way I "am."

So when the church proclaims a belief in and a connection to God, what are we offering the world? Partly we are offering a connection to something beyond ourselves, beyond our ideals, beyond our goals, beyond everything. This is called transcendence. Ultimately God also transcends the church and the Bible, but we can at least proclaim the bits we understand. Hopefully an awareness of transcendence makes us humble, although this is rarely the case. Ideally any attempt to claim to understand the ineffable would only make one look foolish. Too often it is taken for wisdom.

Yet besides a connection to the transcendent God, the church also offers a connection to the innermost reality. This is called immanence. This is the God who is inside rather than outside reality, inside rather than outside language. It is the claim that all these words somehow point us to an initial

Word from which all words derive meaning. This is not the One outside who comes to dwell but the One who is already there.

Yet there is more than connection. Or rather, this connection has multiple parts. It is more than simply a *feeling* of being connected. With (or even without) this feeling comes the many advantages of being in relationship to the source of all being.

A good summary of this is found in Psalm 46:1, 2.

God is our refuge and strength, a very present help in trouble. Therefore we will not fear, though the earth should change, though the mountains shake in the heart of the sea;

When the church offers a connection to God, it is offering a source of help and strength. This connection to God is one thing that distinguishes the church's contribution from those of the many other groups and individuals who are on a similar path. Without in any way denigrating the work of others or suggesting that we have all the answers, the church should be there to connect people with God, a source of strength on the journey. It should be like hanging up a big sign saying "Free Help," as long as we recognize that what we are offering is beyond ourselves. Yes, we will help one another, but there is more. God is that "more."

This also should mean that there can be a certain fearlessness to our work. Here we need to be careful, for I have suggested earlier that we cannot expect God to rescue us from every kind of trouble. But this is quite different from saying that God never rescues.

Psalm 42 also notes that this fearlessness extends to changes in the earth itself. The help being offered through God extends beyond the emotional or spiritual. This is more than the confidence that might arise from a belief that it will all be okay after we die. This is a confidence that comes from loyalty to the one who grounds all of reality and who was present at the beginning and remains present today.

WHY CHURCH?

For the church, the presence of God infuses everything we have been talking about thus far. It is not really fair to call God just another part of what we offer the world. Rather, all the pieces above derive from and are responses to God. God is the One who grounds, motivates, directs, and gives strength to any movement toward the greater good of the world.

In this sense, God is also a vital part of the "we" of "We're all in this together." This may sound strange to some, because so often God is part of

Old Testament—the good news

the problem. Christians (and others) create communities of insiders who exclude and demonize the other side. After all, if you're not on God's side, whose side are you on? But when the understanding of "we" is expanded beyond any particular little group of "us" and expanded further to include all creation, then God not only forms the basis for community but provides strength, grace, and joy to this extended community. God also desires the health of all creation and actively works toward this end. It is certainly possible to do community without acknowledging and accessing the power of God, but why would you?

God can also empower the movement toward contentment. A significant part of faith is trust. To have faith in God is to trust that God will take care of us while somehow also acknowledging that we will suffer and die. So we can and should work on contentment inside ourselves and in our communities, but we can also build contentment on the trust that God can and will provide what is needed.

This is radically difficult work. We can be encouraged by countless stories of times when God has abundantly provided. This is why we need to tell one another the stories of our own experiences. These are the stories that nurture our faith. On the other hand, we also need to remember that the people of God do suffer chronic pain, are killed horribly and tragically, and kill and destroy one another. And for all the stories of people who experience God's presence in the most terrible of circumstances, there are equivalent stories of people who feel abandoned by God. Yet we are called to trust in God. And trust grounds contentment.

The Genesis model we looked at earlier is a story that must include God. It was God who called Abraham, God who brought children to a barren couple, God who promised, and God who spoke and created relationship. On the other hand, this is not a story where God fixed all of Abraham's problems. Abraham needed to journey to Egypt (likely having to fly economy class) because of the famine in the land God had promised. So not only did the promised land have famines but God did nothing miraculous to rescue Abraham. When Abraham got to Egypt, he was afraid of what would happen to him, and he clearly did not expect God to rescue him from the trouble (Genesis 12:10–20).

So again we need to read the story of Genesis with our eyes wide open. The authors of the story are much more honest in telling the story than we may be willing to be when we read it. This is a story of learning to get along, learning to get along even when others don't want to get along, and learning to get along without the guarantee of divine rescue. Yet God does rescue (sometimes). God does call. God does care. Genesis is a story about God, but it is also the story of the God-we-have rather than the God-we-want.

It is this same God who allows for the possibility that our security and confidence for the future are not grounded in military strength. In fact, this seems to be an either/or choice. Either we trust God or we don't. If we don't, we should attempt to secure our future by building up our army. But there are other alternatives. Like we saw in the Genesis story, we could also learn how to get along with each other rather than using deadly force to solve problems. Yet, to a significant degree, our ability to get along should be increased by a trust in God. Again, God is not The Answer to all our problems, but it seems only reasonable to access all available resources when trying to find nonlethal resolutions to conflict. God is available.

Wisdom is also specifically related to God. In a world drowning in fact and opinion, wisdom is what separates the various voices and gleans life-giving, world-sustaining truth. Since life, truth and the world itself are all grounded in God, the Source of wisdom would seem to be a useful ally for anyone seeking wisdom.

In all this, a trust in and loyalty to God also should make it easier to acknowledge and embrace the full range of our emotions. We are what we are. This is no surprise to God. Part of what we are is broken. This is also not a surprise to God. We respond to the world within the confines of our biochemistry, which again is not news to our Creator. God is neither ashamed of nor above our emotions. Attempting to turn God-language into a cold, emotionless description or to rise above our own humanness is not a worthwhile task. God calls us to embrace what and who we are.

THE DANGERS OF GOD-LANGUAGE

Offering people access to the love and power of God may at first appear to be an idea with no flaws. We may even be tempted to enter a fantasy where everyone just loves God and is nice to each other. But being serious about God means that we need turn our brains on rather than off. As quickly as we can, we need to move beyond Santa Claus for adults. We need to do this if for no other reason than that words kill. And words about God also kill.

Many books have been written recently about the death and destruction caused by belief in God. The church needs to take these books seriously. God has been used and continues to be used as an excuse for mass murder, the destruction of entire societies and ecosystems, and the torture and killing of countless "enemies of God." Even inside so-called peace churches, "God" is used to silence and/or exclude certain people. There is lots of guilt to be spread around, so it need not be spread thinly.

There is always a problem in speaking about or for gods. Too often "god" is just a projection of our own desires and ideals. Or, more darkly, "god" is a projection of our fears and hatred. So "god" hates what we hate, which gives us license to hate what God hates and those who hate God (see Psalm 139:21, 22). This is merely the flip side of loving what God loves. In this way, talking about God is just another way of talking about ourselves, without facing up to the truth.

Another problem with god-language is that it becomes a way for believers to take credit for all of the good stuff that happens. When our army defeats theirs, it is because of God. When someone is healed, it is God at work. Even when atheists are successful, believers claim it is God secretly at work. So while others strive for wisdom and truth, we already possess it. And when people seek answers, we have the Answer. Thinking this way is a real temptation. It leads to a self-important, pompous church. It does not lead naturally to humility.

STILL

Our inability to comprehend God does not mean the task is pointless, only that it needs to be accompanied by honest humility. The insufficiency of language is also not a reason to abandon God, because the same can be said about love. Love is also beyond language, but that is no reason to abandon the idea of love. There is something else out there and in here. We can pretend there isn't, but why would we?

This is especially true when we are trying to accomplish something. There are countless tasks worthy of human effort—alleviating suffering, the survival of the human species and other species, joy, beauty, and peace. In each of these efforts, God is an advocate and a source of strength. Even thinking about this at the most utilitarian level, why turn down free help?

So the church reaches out and tries to be part of the solution to the problems of the world. In doing this, it could proclaim a theologically sophisticated doctrine of the omni-whatever Deity. Or it could, honestly and humbly, offer what it has and what it is, while proclaiming, watching, and listening for the voice and action of God. This sounds like a fairly easy choice on the surface but has proved difficult in practice. Hopefully we will keep practicing.

5

The New Testament—the good news

a) Development of Old Testament themes

THUS FAR WE HAVE been looking at some of the basic ideas in the Old Testament that could form the basis for the church's proclamation of the good news. If the gospel is, at its most basic level, a message of salvation, then it must have something to contribute to the ongoing search for health, wholeness, and ultimately the survival of the planet. The church does not undertake this task alone. There are countless other individuals and groups who are trying to find and foster salvation. Yet hopefully the church has something to offer.

For Christians, of course, much of the message of salvation comes to us through the New Testament, in the words of and about Jesus of Nazareth. So this chapter will focus on the New Testament, initially asking what the New Testament adds to the themes we have already noted, then later looking at new themes and ideas.

In doing this, we need to recognize that the New Testament is itself a collection. It does not speak with a single voice, but offers us a conversation. Mark's understanding of Jesus is slightly different from Matthew's, both of which are different from Luke's, and all three of which are quite different from John or Paul or the writer of Hebrews. The New Testament places these various voices in the same collection, but it is not helpful to simply state that the all have "basically" the same message. So in this study, we will listen to the various voices as they speak of each theme and ultimately speak of salvation.

The New Testament—the good news

A) WE'RE ALL IN THIS TOGETHER

Despite the individualist turn in most Euro-Western societies, the New Testament is still basically a community-oriented document. This is hardly surprising, since first-century Mediterranean societies had no real concept of the individual. People gained their identity on the basis of belonging to a group. They thought of themselves like fingers on a hand. Each finger is its own thing, but has no purpose or function or life if not attached to a hand.

The community was also a multilayered thing. People were parts of families, clans, and tribes, each group encompassing a larger number of people. Within this system, it is also helpful to remember that being Jewish was an ethnic identity, rather than a religious or national one. To claim to be Jewish spoke of who your parents were, what you ate, where you lived (i.e. in the Jewish part of town), and how you acted. Certain beliefs were often part of this larger identity but were not strictly necessary. "Jewish atheist" was not an oxymoron, although it would have been rare.

As the teachings and example of Jesus continued to be followed after his death, it became something apart from mainstream Jewish identity. This "something" was not the same in every place, but in many places it did result in separation from family. For people of that world, religious identity was ethnic identity. So changing the first meant losing the second. This meant that people, when joining the Jesus movement, often lost their basic identity. This must have caused a major crisis for many of them. In response, the church became a substitute identity, that of "Christian." This gave people a sense of self that was not necessarily connected to geography, biology, race, or empire.

Of course, this was not always the case. Sometimes whole families joined the Jesus movement. People did not cease being from somewhere or part of the Roman empire. So the identity of this new "we" in the church has always existed in tension with other forms of group identity. Some, like Paul himself, were both Jewish and Christian, and saw no conflict between these. Others were both Christian and Ethiopian, both Christian and Roman citizens, or both Christian and Celtic.

As we try to bring this tension into a postmodern society, we find that commitment to the church becomes part of a mélange of identities for many people. The tension between competing or overlapping loyalties often felt in modernist societies is becoming the new normal. Few people have a single center to their selves that overrides all other loyalties. Many organizations, such as the church and the nation, still claim ultimate loyalty from members, but even this is simply compartmentalized by people claiming this. So Americans are ultimately loyal to America over other *nations* but not over every other group loyalty. Christians may proclaim loyalty to Jesus over every other *religion* but again not over everything. "Ultimate" is not as ultimate as it used to be.

What this means is that the church is both more and less than it used to be. Loss of ultimate loyalty means that the church is no longer the center of most people's lives as it was for many, but it also means that fewer people are willing to kill for their church. It also means that the influence of the teachings of Jesus may be less among the faithful but greater among those outside the formal church. Jesus is no longer controlled or contained by the church, and neither are Christians.

Thus, in postmodern societies, the "we" of "we're all in this together" includes the influence of Jesus and the New Testament in entirely new ways. Yet in some small way this is made possible by the movement in the early church away from the usual sorts of identity of their societies. From the beginning, loyalty to Jesus was incorporated into various forms of identity. The teachings of Jesus have little difficulty transcending ethnic, national, and even religious loyalty because the New Testament was written by and for people attempting to do just that.

This means both loss of direct influence and gain of indirect influence for the church. It sets the church free from other systems that attempt to contain its radical teachings. It allows the church to proclaim without needing to claim that it has all the answers. Jesus is free to be the center of the church as well as a Jewish rabbi, a Muslim prophet, and a great teacher, and the church can be part of a much larger dialogue without trying to dominate the discussion.

B) CONTENTMENT

As we saw in the Old Testament section, contentment promotes a set of priorities that are paradoxical. On the one hand, we are called and encouraged to be content with enough for survival and occasional feasting, but neither strive for nor desire more than that. After all, if some have more than they need, others will have less. On the other hand, we are not to be content with injustice, with the suffering of others, with oppression, or with sin.

The New Testament negotiates this contentment/discontentment paradox in a variety of ways, depending on where we are reading. For example,

The New Testament—the good news

Matthew records Jesus as saying many things about being satisfied with enough. In the Sermon on the Mount (Matthew 5-7), Jesus taught about the value of not worrying even about what we eat or what we wear, because God provides (Matthew 6:25-34). This attitude is reinforced in the Lord's Prayer, where we ask for "our daily bread" (Matthew 6:11), sufficient for the day without worrying about bread for tomorrow. This is one of those passages that is known by people around the world, yet I wonder how many people can even imagine doing it. Throw away your refrigerator, empty your kitchen cupboards and your pantry, and trust God to feed you today with no thought of what you will eat tomorrow. As Jesus said, "Tomorrow will bring worries of its own" (Matthew 6:34).

On the other hand, Matthew also records many times when Jesus was less than content with the way things were. In Matthew, Jesus mostly focused on the Pharisees (see Matthew 23:13-36), whom he called all sorts of nasty things. These sayings are often tricky for the modern church, since they can either become part of anti-Jewish polemic, or they can be understood as general condemnations of religious leaders. However we choose to understand these sayings, they are clearly not those of someone who was content with the current state of the world.

In Mark, the focus is different. Whatever it is that Jesus said about contentment, Mark's picture of Jesus is not of someone who models contentment. Jesus was constantly rushing around doing things, not sitting still long enough to be a good example of being satisfied. On the other hand, Jesus is also shown as without concern for his own needs because he was focused on the needs of others and the proclamation of the kingdom of God.

Part of the difference between Matthew and Mark is their central focus. Matthew focuses on identity—the emerging identity of the Jesus movement after the destruction of Jerusalem. Mark, on the other hand, has no central focus but is certainly concerned with the issue of purity. Purity was an important issue in Judaism and the early church because it involved separation from an evil world in an attempt to draw closer to a holy God. The flip side of purity is that it also so easily divides those inside the community. It separates those able to maintain purity codes (usually wealthy, land-owning men) from the many who simply cannot (women, the poor, slaves). In a society where roughly 90 percent of Jewish people would fall into one of the latter categories, purity was an ideal that separated the few from the many.

You Are Not Going to Heaven (and why it doesn't matter)

When purity overlaps with contentment (in the form of smugness), there is little room for compassion. Purity separates the pure from the impure. When we become content in our purity, we lose the ability to love those who are "not as good as we are." Jesus confronts this regularly when he eats with sinners, tax collectors, and other "impure" people. He is often condemned for this by the Pharisees, the guardians of purity. Compassion, on the other hand, connects people. Mark shows Jesus always choosing compassion over purity.

This will continue to be a major issue in the early church. The letters of John and the book of Revelation proclaim purity as an important goal for Christians—both purity of belief and purity of action. Mark's Gospel strongly disagrees, for it continues to highlight inclusion rather than the exclusion that comes from purity. For our purposes here, this is important because purity and true contentment are not easily compatible. The constant vigilance that purity demands does not lead easily to contentment.

Luke's picture of Jesus highlights the economic aspects of contentment. But Luke does not highlight the idea of being content with the way things are. He believes that the system is broken and needs to be fixed. So while Luke includes Jesus' suggestion to "consider the lilies" (12:27), this section on contentment proclaims that concern about money and possessions is a major stumbling block for those who seek the kingdom of God.

People have often noted that an economic system grounded in the teachings of Jesus is unlikely to succeed in a larger social system. This is hardly surprising, given that Jesus' system requires contentment. The economics of the kingdom must be embraced and joyfully chosen, rather than imposed by a central authority. It is difficult to imagine how someone would legislate contentment.

When the early church attempted to embrace the teachings of Jesus, it did not require everyone to fit the same pattern. This is the point of the Ananias and Sapphira story in Acts 5. Peter was clear that the couple was free to keep their land or use the proceeds from the sale as they saw fit (5:4), but instead they lied about the price of the land. These were not the actions of people who had embraced the values of the kingdom and were content with the decisions they had made.

One of the questions that received various answers in the early church was the one about the basis of contentment. That is, in a world of suffering, disease, oppression, and persecution, how can anyone proclaim contentment as a central value? This question became more pressing as time went

The New Testament—the good news

on, given Jesus' refusal to return and set up God's kingdom using divine power. After all, if Jesus would return and we could be fed by heavenly manna while basking in the glory of God as special deputies of the Son, contentment would be rather easy. Contentment is always easy when we're lying on a beach relaxing with a cool drink. But the early church had little opportunity to bask in the glory of being God's special people.

Instead, the church remained a minor group on the edges of both Jewish and Roman society, sometimes tolerated, occasionally persecuted but never outwardly treated as the chosen ones of God. In many ways, this is the journey of Paul. Paul was called by a vision from God and given a specific mission. He knew himself to be one given both mission and authority to proclaim the message of Jesus, the savior whose imminent return would herald the new age. As time went on, however, Paul found himself an oft-persecuted and maligned father to a bunch of scrappy little gatherings who spent more time battling internal and external foes (and friends) than they did living out the mission they had been given.

Yet despite the gulf that existed between his early expectation and his later reality, Paul managed to preach a gospel of contentment. It is something he learned along the way (Philippians 4:11). Anyone who reads his letters will quickly discover that being content did not come easily to Paul. He was often angry, contentious, frustrated, exasperated, argumentative, and harsh. And we know this despite the fact that we probably don't have a copy of the angry letter he sent to the church in Corinth (see 2 Corinthians 7:8).

So Paul found contentment (eventually), and he found it in the oddest place. He did not find it despite his circumstances but because of them. He learned to ground himself not in God-who-will-rescue-me but in the God who was glorified in his weakness and suffering (2 Corinthians 12:10). This made his personal circumstances irrelevant to his basic outlook on life. After all, he was the apostle of the suffering one, the crucified and risen savior.

Even more than this, Paul learned to move beyond contentment to joy. Or rather, he held the two together. He was even willing to go so far as to proclaim suffering as part of joy, for it proclaimed his participation in the redemption of the world (Colossians 1:24).[4]

In all of this, the New Testament proclaims a paradoxical contentment, an attitude of joy that nevertheless willingly suffers with and for the

---

4. Colossians may not have been written by Paul, but this verse is in line with a number of Paul's other statements on suffering.

world around it. This is not just part of the proclamation of the church, but is its mission. This is not a church that sits comfortably in the center of town and tells the world around it how to live. This is the church on the margins of society, made up of those who joyfully and willingly embrace the suffering-yet-triumphant God. The church does not aspire to more than this because there is nothing that is "more" than living out the good news.

C) THE GENESIS MODEL

It follows logically from the previous sections that the Joshua model of conquest and slaughter is not an option for followers of Jesus. Given the way identity is constructed without reference to land or ethnicity, it is difficult to imagine how a group of Christians could, as Christians, lay claim to a specific piece of land. This becomes even more obvious with the radically open "us" created by the postmodern turn. Conquest and slaughter are also not an option for people who embrace the truth that suffering may be endured for the sake of others, but is not to be deliberately caused by us.

This can also be seen when we understand the message and ministry of Jesus as a use of the Genesis model. Jesus lived in a society where the people of God, living on the land God promised them, were under the authority of the Roman empire. Yet there is little evidence in the Gospels or elsewhere that Jesus engaged in direct conflict with the Romans. It is the word "direct" that is crucial here, since there is much evidence that he was in indirect conflict with the Romans, the most obvious sign being his death on a cross.

It is also important to remember that much of his conflict was with the Pharisees and the Temple authorities in Jerusalem. These groups were also attempting to negotiate life in the face of Roman authority and oppression. Apparently their vision of how to do this was different from Jesus' program.

Gospels

When we look more specifically at the Gospels, we can see various ways that Jesus' life was understood in conflict with the Exodus/Joshua model of dealing with others. In Mark, a significant problem is that the people are primed for the Exodus/Joshua model. This is part of the explanation for what is called the "messianic secret," in which Jesus continued to tell people not to tell others about him. If people believed Jesus was the Messiah, their

The New Testament—the good news

likely reaction would have been to prepare for military confrontation. This had already happened around the time of Jesus' birth, and would happen again thirty-five years after his death. So if Jesus was attempting to start a direct confrontation with the Romans, he had easy ways to do this. Instead, in Mark the idea of "Messiah" needs to be redefined. Jesus is still declared to be Messiah, the one who saves, yet this is presented in the context of the Messiah who also died at the hands of the Romans.

Mark's picture of Jesus contains a clear warning to anyone who would champion the Genesis model. Some people are not interested in getting along, and confronting them could get you killed. In this scenario, the empty tomb serves as a double sign. It demonstrates God's approval of the way of Jesus, but it paradoxically stands as a symbol of what will likely *not* happen to us if we confront an oppressive system. The movement may continue and be strengthened, but we may be dead.

Matthew presents the Jesus paradigm in a different way. In Matthew, Jesus was the new Moses. We see this in the numerous parallels between the birth of Jesus as told by Matthew and the story of Moses. Jesus was the one who was delivered from the death squads of a fearful tyrant, came out of Egypt, and proclaimed the law of God on a mountain. But Matthew is also clear that Jesus also transformed the message and the mission of Moses. This was a new way, and the new law was not simply a replacement for the old one.

In these and other ways, in the Gospels the Exodus/Joshua model is overwritten by the Genesis model. The Exodus model privileges a rather simple and straightforward response to enemies—either let God kill them or do it yourself. Jesus' alternative was not just to learn to get along but to love your enemies, an active response of positive engagement. This is neither simple nor straightforward.

Another way to understand Jesus and the Genesis model is to think about the daily realities of his life. Jesus and his disciples wandered into a village in Galilee. Since visiting rabbis may have be relatively rare events, and since there was nothing else to do after the sun went down (Galilee having limited wifi coverage in the first century), the people of the village would naturally have gathered in the evenings to listen to what this person had to say. What did he say? While the Gospels often fill this gap with the frustrating phrase, "and Jesus taught the crowds," we can piece some of this together from what we do know. Did he call the whole village to abandon their land and wander with him? There is no indication that he did, and besides, what would have been the point? A wandering band of a thousand is simply not sustainable, and what makes wandering more holy than farming?

Thus, Jesus' message of the "kingdom of God" must have somehow been relevant to subsistence farmers who were likely still recovering from the effects of the revolt of 4 BC. Significant parts of the population had been killed or wounded in the revolt or sold into slavery afterward. The villages were also paying for the reconstruction of the cities through taxes.

So "learning to get along" here becomes vital. This would have included learning to get along inside the village. It is often much easier to love enemies than family, especially in times of social and economic stress. Does the village work together to survive, or is it every family for themselves? If one family prospers, how does this affect the rest of the village?

These villagers also needed to figure out how to live in relation with the Roman/Herodian authorities. The Joshua strategy had proved very unsuccessful last time. Was it time for a new way, or was the need for survival so overwhelming that there was no room for anything more? And when these people heard about the coming "kingdom of God," was it the way of the God of Moses and Joshua they thought of or the way of the God of Abraham?

So Jesus spoke his message to people who still lived with the experience of an unsuccessful attempt to replicate the Exodus/Joshua model of dealing with others. His proclamation of the coming kingdom was not part of that model but looked more like the Genesis model. The early church also saw a further attempt to enact the Exodus/Joshua model in the revolt of 66 AD, which led directly to the destruction of the Jerusalem temple in 70 AD. So it is not surprising that they remembered their Messiah as proclaiming a different way, a way more suited to a small group attempting to survive in an overwhelming and often hostile empire. Obviously God had shown that the big divine rescue was not going to happen according to human timetables, so the way forward must look different from that.

Paul

The life and letters of Paul also demonstrate a particular expression of the Genesis model. Paul's model, of course, is fundamentally apocalyptic. At least early on in his work, he expected Jesus to return soon to do the power-and-might thing. So his churches did not need a long-term strategy for getting along. But there are still resources in Paul's writings that can be helpful for people who do need a more long-term approach to living in a world where God does not rescue them from all their problems.

We see this best when we realize that much of Paul's language is as much political as it is spiritual. We so easily assume that words like "faith" and "peace" and "saved" are religious terms. They were certainly words that related to the whole "God thing," but for Paul, *everything* related to the God thing. This was also true for the Roman Empire, where the power and peace and salvation brought (in their own minds) by the Roman empire were expressions of the victory of their gods over those of others.

So while Paul appreciated the relative peace and safety that allowed him to travel about the Roman world, he found safety and security not in the Roman empire but in God (1 Thessalonians 5:3). And he placed his faith/trust/loyalty (all good translations of the Greek word *pistis*) in God rather than in human authorities. This is despite the many times that God failed to rescue him from danger and possible death (see the list in 2 Corinthians 11:23–27). So while Paul did not experience the return of Jesus that he spoke of in 1 Thessalonians 5, or the rescue of Jesus from his many difficulties, he did not abandon his loyalty to a vision of one human family that lives in peace.

Paul went beyond this vision and also understood his own suffering as part of God's work of salvation. This was a step beyond just-get-along and involved bringing about a new way of relating to one another. His hope and his faith was that this is best done "in Christ" (Galatians 3:28) and inside God's covenant with Abraham (Galatians 3:29), and that prior to the return of Jesus this involves relating to others as "those who are perishing" (1 Corinthians 1:18) rather than "those we need to kill."

D) LIMITS AND WARNINGS ABOUT MILITARISM

Once again, the New Testament's response to this theme follows logically from the previous themes. The way of suffering love, when coupled with a hope for the salvation of the world, leads obviously to a place where military strength is more of a hindrance than a help in reaching our goals.

This is also not surprising, given historical parallels between first-century Galilee and the time of Persian rule. Like the Jews living under Persian domination, Jesus lived in an occupied territory. When he was a small boy, the Romans reconquered the area around Nazareth after a brief uprising by the people. In reprisal for the uprising, they killed thousands of people, crucified thousands more, and sent many away into slavery. Likely his parents knew people who were killed or taken away by the Roman invaders.

The Romans continued to occupy Galilee, and Jesus grew up under their rule. One of the main ways the Romans kept the people from rebellion was to crucify those who were suspected of leading resistance movements. Crosses were placed at major intersections as a continual reminder of the punishment awaiting those who chose to resist Roman rule. The opposite of the cross was the sword. The cross was for losers; the sword for winners.

So it must have been shocking to hear Jesus' call for his followers to take up the cross (Matthew 10:38). His disciples might have anticipated a call to take up the sword, to take back the land God had given them, and to fight for freedom and liberty. Jesus did call the disciples to freedom, to the battle against evil. His weapon of choice, however, was the cross, the enemy's symbol of suffering and humiliation.

We have lost the radical nature of this challenge by making the cross a pretty little thing that is worn as jewelry or used as decoration. Imagine instead wearing a gold electric chair on a chain around your neck, or thumb screws used as dangling earrings. Instead of taking up the suffering of the world as a symbol of their identity, the modern church has too often become a defender of the right of empire to torture and kill.

The early church understood Jesus' challenge as a call to break with the violence of the world around them. They resisted violence with love. Many fled to the deserts, giving up everything they had, rather than be conscripted into the army. For the first 300 years, the church walked Jesus' path of peace in a violent and hostile world.

Paul

Imagine that one of your child's teachers is teaching about the importance of obeying the law. This teacher often speaks directly about the importance of good government and the duties of law-abiding citizens. Now imagine that one day you hear this teacher boasting about how much time he has spent in jail and how many times he has come into conflict with the law. Likely you would wonder what kind of message this teacher is really giving the students.

This is exactly the situation we find when we study the letters of Paul. In Romans 13:1–7, we find Paul telling the church in Rome to be obedient to the governing authorities and stressing the importance of good conduct before the law. Yet over in 2 Corinthians 11:21–29, he boasts about the imprisonments, floggings, and lashes he received at the hands of various authorities, considering these things to be signs of true apostleship. How are we to understand this mixed message?

Apparently Paul believed there were certain exceptions to the idea of following the law. Obviously for Paul the exception was when he had to choose between following God and obeying the law. Paul understood clearly the difference between rules made by humans and rules made by God (see Peter's declaration in Acts 5:29). That is why he told the Romans to be subject to the governing authorities—not always obedient but willing to live with the consequences of disobedience, following the example of Jesus on the cross.

Paul likely grew up in a wealthy home, surrounded by material comfort and a life of ease made possible by slave labor. He had the opportunity to study under one of the most important teachers of his day. He benefited from the Roman system of law and order, the *Pax Romana* (Roman peace) made possible by the ever-present reminders of military power.

So the logical way forward for Paul was either to embrace the Roman system of power through strength, or oppose it through counter-violence as an agent of the Exodus/Joshua model. Alternatively, he could have used the Genesis model of just learning to get along with the Gentile world around him. Instead, he moved beyond either model to a new goal of including these Gentiles and even the Roman soldiers in the community of salvation. Whatever limited role Paul saw for human soldiers (such as keeping the roads free from bandits), he could never have imagined a future where Christian soldiers would march forward and impose or even defend belief with the sword.

As a follower of Jesus, Paul was freed from his bondage to the system that supported his status and position. He became a tentmaker, a lowly job that helped him identify with the poor and the slaves. He was shown the way of suffering, the way of making peace. This was more than a religious conversion; it was a social and political conversion as well.

E) WISDOM

As we saw in the section on the Old Testament and wisdom, wisdom walks the path of tradition. Highlighting wisdom means reverence for the advice of our elders, a preference for the way things have always been done, and a sense of continuity and stability in our communities. While this path is well-trodden in many churches today, it did not fit comfortably with the realities of the early church.

In fact, wisdom was a problem for the early church. Wisdom is the way of tradition, the way of honoring parents and the traditions of the elders. It was the way of the priests and the Pharisees, who saw their task as upholding tradition and even expanding tradition into all parts of life. These were also the groups with whom Jesus and his disciples came into conflict. In that sense, Jesus was more of an anti-wisdom figure than a teacher of tradition.

This remained a major problem for the early church. This is especially true because they lived in a world that revered tradition. Both the Jewish and the Roman world honored the old way of doing things. This was a world where "new" was a suspicious adjective. People did not generally want the newest product or idea or way of doing something. They recognized stability and constancy as virtues. Imagine people who are proud of their dial telephones, openly mocking those who have iPhones. This was the general thinking of most in the ancient world. So when the church proclaimed the way of Jesus, it was not to their advantage to highlight the newness of his teaching.

Matthew is the Gospel that deals with this reality most directly. Matthew thinks of Jesus as the new Moses, which allows him to highlight both the connection with tradition and the new thing that is happening. He also talks constantly about the fulfillment of prophecy, thus demonstrating how the new thing is actually in continuity with the old thing.

Paul had a more complex problem in the Greco-Roman world. His future-oriented apocalyptic ideas did not sell well in a society based in tradition. The Greeks also had entire systems of thought and speech based on specific philosophical ideas of wisdom, which placed Paul in direct competition with the leading thinkers of his day. In presenting his own ideas, Paul placed himself in direct competition with these systems. Whatever Paul thought he was doing, his listeners in the cities would have placed his teachings in the context of rival philosophical systems.

In addition to the competition, Paul's problem was that philosophical systems were not his strength. However much modern Christians want to see Paul as the great theologian, in his own world his presentation and style were clearly second-rate. He even admits this in his letters (2 Corinthians

The New Testament—the good news

10:10). It may be that Apollos had the training and presence to sound like a teacher of wisdom, but not Paul.

So Paul offered an alternative. He contrasted human wisdom with God's wisdom (see 1 Corinthians 2). For Paul, this wisdom from God was not found most clearly in tradition or in philosophical argument. God's wisdom was revealed in the cross. Paul understood that this was a foolish argument (1 Corinthians 2:14), and for obvious reasons. Imagine claiming that God and all reality is best understood by looking at the hangman's noose and further that one should look at the noose from the perspective of its victims. Who would take that argument seriously? This is why Paul's churches were mostly filled with people from the bottom of society rather than with wealthy men and philosophers.

So the category of wisdom as the patient application of tradition is not one easily derived from the New Testament. The Messiah has come. The kingdom of God is coming. God has come to earth in the flesh. This same Savior is about to be revealed to the whole world. What the prophets of old only dimly foresaw has finally arrived.

All this places the postmodern church in an odd position. We are inheritors of this message of new-and-improved, a significantly anti-tradition message. On the other hand, we are inheritors of a 2,000-year-old tradition. Parts of it are more recent, but often these modern movements attempt to connect themselves to the original message of Jesus and the church. So what does one do with a 2,000-year-old message of new-and-improved? In a world where many things are out of date as soon as they are manufactured and where scientific papers have been superseded before they get published, how do we offer an ancient text and tradition as something worthy of anything other than historical curiosity?

So we come around back to wisdom. In order for the Bible to play the role of wisdom for the postmodern world, we need to demonstrate respect for tradition. The church needs to be the place where we slow down. It is the gathering of people who calmly look back in order to look forward. The Bible is our tradition, our ancient Word of God. In some sense, this whole book is about the role of wisdom, for this is the role of the Bible.

In this focus on wisdom, it is also helpful to recognize the slightly schizophrenic and comical nature of our enterprise. We want to sing a new song unto the Lord, but who else uses the word "unto"? We use our computers and tablets to read and study a text that is older than the idea of the book. We abandon traditional churches for ones with worship bands and pastors in blue jeans, while still trying to find answers in ancient Greek and Hebrew manuscripts. Even as we move toward the new and improved, we continue to be drawn to tradition.

This needs to be celebrated. The church that can't laugh at itself deserves to fade into history. Tradition and comedy are both ways of looking at the world from new perspectives. They both function to break us out of our rigid thought patterns and open us to what is unfolding. Tradition does not lock us in because tradition is always open to new interpretations.

We can't go back, but we need not simply duplicate either the past or the present. In fact, we cannot duplicate the past, and the present will change as it continues to become the past. The challenge before us is to re-read our tradition as new revelation. Reading the old story of the great new thing while smiling at the foolishness of it all seems like a good place to start.

F) EMOTIONS

In many churches, when the Bible is read, it is all read in the same flat, emotionless tone. So "May the God of hope fill you with all joy and peace" (Romans 15:13) is read in the same tone as "Jesus began to weep" (John 11:35), which is indistinguishable in tone from Paul's desire that his opponents castrate themselves (Galatians 5:12). In this way, the emotions that are clearly there in the words are lost in the reading.

Scholarship is also part of the problem. The Bible is usually read with an eye to history or theology, not to emotions. Scholars also tend to write without much emotion, for in academia emotion is contrasted with logic and logic is thought of as superior. Pastors, who are often trained by scholars and who consult scholars in preparing sermons, are then also inclined to see the logical rather than the emotional content of the text. This can result in long, largely humorless sermons on joy or emotionless discussions of emotion (like this one).

For many readers of the Bible, the classic emotion is guilt. The Bible is too often read as a book of rules. These are rules that cannot be followed perfectly, and perfection is the only standard allowed. The response to failure is the feeling of guilt, which may or may not be relieved through various prayers or rituals. Somehow this is regarded as "salvation."

So it comes as a surprise to many people that there is not a lot of feeling guilty in the New Testament. There, guilt is not a feeling; neither is repentance. Guilt is a state of being—something you are or are not—and repentance involves doing right rather than wrong. So at the end of Peter's sermon to the people of Jerusalem after Pentecost (Acts 2, 3), the people recognized their sin in crucifying Jesus, were "cut to the heart," and responded, "Brothers, what should we *do*?" (Acts 2:37). If we understand this passage as an idealized response to the gospel, the response to the recognition of guilt is action.

This is not to suggest that there were no emotions involved in this scene. No doubt Peter's sermon was passionate, and the response was equally emotion-filled. What we also need to see, however, is that nowhere does Peter recommend an ongoing *feeling* of guilt. Rather, the church is described in this way: "They broke bread at home and ate their food with glad and generous hearts, praising God and having the goodwill of all the people" (Acts 2:46, 47). This is not a description of people laden down with feelings of guilt but of a people set free.

When we read the New Testament without a general haze of guilt, we find a wide range of emotions. Much of this is lost in translation across culture. The Gospels were likely originally written largely to aid the memory of those who presented the good news as oral performance. The speaker would have inserted emotion into the words of Jesus as a natural part of good presentation. We seldom encounter people trained in oral performance in the church and can read the Bible for ourselves without hearing the emotions embedded in the stories and letters. This means the text was written without noting emotion because the emotion was supplied by the reader/performer.

Even so, it is not difficult to imagine the emotions behind some of Jesus' words. It is difficult to imagine Jesus saying, "Woe to you, scribes and Pharisees, hypocrites" (Matthew 23:15), without significant emotion. The cleansing of the temple must have been an emotional event. Jesus spoke directly about emotions at various points in his sermons. The parables must have been presented in a memorable way (or they would not have been remembered), which implies emotional display.

Paul more obviously displays his feelings in his letters. He was alternately joyful and angry, frustrated and hopeful, depending on the situation. The Thessalonian church received long sections of thanksgiving (1 Thessalonians 1:2—3:13), and the church in Philippi heard about Paul's joy (Philippians 1:4), while the churches in Galatia had Paul spitting fire (see Galatians 1:6), and the church in Corinth received an angry letter from Paul that caused them grief (note all the emotions mentioned in 2 Corinthians 7).

Paul also speaks of God's emotions. This is a bit trickier to describe, for words about attitudes (mercy, grace) are linked to emotions, but the link is not always clear. In general, Paul saw God in bipolar terms—either love or wrath. Yet it is God's mercy that constantly seeks to find ways to avoid wrath.

It is this whole range of emotions that allows us to read the Bible as a book about real events and real people. These people are like us yet different. But like us, they are whole. The Bible is not a book about perfect saints, full of rules for how the rest of us are to live a life of guilt. When we allow the love and the anger to spill out of the text, we can become more comfortable with our own humanity, both the good and the evil. This also means that salvation can be found within our humanity rather than apart from it.

G) GOD

Depending on whom you listen to, the New Testament adds much or nothing to what the Old Testament proclaims about God. This is reflected in our knowledge of the early church, where some churches found their belief in Jesus to be in simple continuity with their Scriptures (i.e. the Old Testament), while others thought that Jesus revealed a different God entirely. Both points of view have scriptures that can be quoted and analyzed in support of their positions.

The real problem for the modern church is that all this quickly becomes theology. That is, we can and do discuss ideas about God and perhaps attempt to draw implications from various theological assertions, but it is difficult imagining any of this discussion becoming anything more than discussion. So the church becomes another voice in the marketplace of ideas, mostly competing with other churches for market share.

I am not suggesting that ideas don't matter. The church potentially offers major critiques and alternatives to many of the foundational beliefs and myths of our societies. Reading the Gospels with eyes wide open allows us to recognize the impact of consumerism and militarism on our entire worldview and presents a challenge to these and other ideological commitments.

But the God question is more than that. How do we move from thinking about God to acting with God? How do we move from ideas about God to experiences of God? How do we move from belief in God to participating in the will of God? In other words, how does the church spend less time offering the world ideas about God and more time offering the world *God?*

In attempting to answer this question, I want to highlight two significant ways the New Testament characters and writers relate to God.

Father/Parent

The first comes directly from the words of Jesus. Jesus spoke often about relating to God as Father. I realize this gendered metaphor potentially causes as many problems as it solves, but if we can forgive Jesus for attempting to provide a culturally appropriate metaphor, we can also be free to construct our own metaphors on the foundation he has provided.

I say "culturally appropriate" because of how Jesus' social world worked. Fathers were the heads of the household. This was always true in theory, no matter how much it was not true in practice. It was one of those ideas that everyone needed to pretend to believe. So if Jesus had called God his mother, everyone would immediately have wondered who was greater than God. Who was playing the father role?

This cultural appropriateness means that in order to convey what Jesus meant we can no longer exclusively use "father" language. The English word "father" does not mean the same as either the Aramaic (Jesus' original language) *abba* or the Greek word *pater*. While it refers to the same group of people, the roles and attitudes assumed in these terms do not match. Lacking any English word equivalent to *abba* or *pater*, I am going to use "parent" as an imperfect substitute. This should not be particularly distressing, since all language for God is imperfect at best.

In order to understand the radical new way of relating to God that is opened up by this metaphor, we need to keep in mind the traditional alternatives. People in Jesus' day, both Jews and others, usually related to the gods as distant beings, residing in temples or on mountains. This made the gods generally unapproachable. The gods may or may not have heard what you said, and they may have responded, but one was always aware of the gulf that separates us and them. Much of this was just as true in Judaism as it was in surrounding cultures.

Parents, of course, are much closer. While still commanding honor and fidelity, they are regularly nearby. They are aware of the situation of each individual in the household and are affected by things that happen in the family.

All this, of course, remains metaphor. No matter how much our language about God reflects presence and intimacy, God is not physically present. If you leave an empty chair at the table for God to sit in, God regularly fails to eat the food.

Still, prayer to "Parent God" has a potential intimacy that prayer to "God who sits enthroned in the heavens" does not. The remaining issue is what we do with this potential. Believing that God is near, that God cares and is interested in our lives, can lead to many attitudes and actions. We could use the practice of prayer to Parent God to increase our self-centeredness and destructive pride. We could decide that since God is our Parent, then God loves us more than others. We could begin to believe that those who are suffering are just not as holy as we are, because God our/their father is not pleased with them. We could begin to act as if all our actions are approved by our Parent God, and that no standard exists outside our own ambition or ideology. And certainly we can use this newfound connection to reinforce patriarchal patterns of action.

So offering the world a deeper connection to God is at best a mixed blessing. This is especially true within the context of empire, where self-centered pride is often the most natural place to begin. Church history is filled with examples of human empires that torture, kill, and destroy entire cultures while claiming the blessing of God, based on their intimacy with God. Family histories are also filled with stories of human fathers who claim the authority of Father God to destroy the bodies and minds of the women and girls around them.

These things must be named. These stories must be told. Somehow Christians have regularly moved from suffering *for* others to causing suffering *to* others. This temptation is built into any theology that claims a special relationship to the divine. There is only a short distance between "I am on God's side" and "God is on my side."

This is especially problematic in a culture that refuses to acknowledge its inherent polytheism. If we could be honest about the variety of things that we worship and be able to speak clearly about the choices, there would be less temptation to conflate the options, to pretend that all these gods are one.

Holy Spirit

In most ways, talking about the Spirit of God is not significantly different from the previous section. This is especially true when we want to think about the relationship between faith and the survival of the planet. Somehow I doubt that the health of the planet is directly or even indirectly related to a correct set of doctrines about the nature of God. So we are going to try to talk about the Holy Spirit without worrying about whether you or

I or anyone else can make sense out of trinitarian doctrine (the idea that God is three-in-one).

In that same vein, we also need to understand that the Spirit is not something that the church is offering to the world. Rather, the Spirit is God's offering to the world. In chapter 4(g), I said that the idea of God in the Old Testament is not simply the idea of God, but an offer of assistance, like putting out a sign saying, "Free Help." In this same way, the language of the Holy Spirit is God's way of saying, "Yes, really, I want to help."

This also needs to be coupled with the realization that God has desires for the world. Getting this part right is really important. If we believe God is offering help without realizing that God's help has a particular direction to it, we risk another encounter with the God-we-want. Within this scheme, the Holy Spirit then becomes the heavenly vending machine, portable edition. Thus God not only gives us everything we want but follows us around to make sure we get it when we want it.

Or not. Perhaps continuing with mass killing and environmental devastation is not something God is going to help with. This is not to suggest that the Spirit is going to save us if we choose to pursue this course. It is merely to say that, if we want the help of the Spirit, then we need to act within the will of God.

Once we get beyond this basic notion of the active presence of God, we see that the New Testament is not particularly worried about exactly who or what the Spirit is and so offers us a variety of ways of talking and thinking about how God is present among us. This is because, in general, the New Testament is oriented to the practical rather than the theoretical. And this is because the writers of the New Testament were more concerned with survival than with developing abstract systems. So in a world more in need of survival than philosophy, the New Testament regains the status of practical guide rather than theological textbook.

Even within the Gospels, there are different ways of understanding the ongoing presence of God. It is always important to remember that in many ways the writers of the New Testament are making this stuff up as they go along. Jesus came, the expected-yet-unexpected Messiah. Jesus died, rose again, and left, all without lengthy explanation. Groups of Jesus' followers started meeting and tried to figure out, What now?

Within these meetings, they also experienced the presence of God in some unexpected ways. They had these experiences as they met, as they went about their lives, and as they wrote to one another. Living as they did in a

You Are Not Going to Heaven (and why it doesn't matter)

world where the spirit world was always intimately connected to the physical world, they called these experiences the Holy Spirit or the Spirit of God. They understood this to be in continuity with the work and message of Jesus.

Mark and Matthew don't have a lot to say about this spirit. John the Baptist predicts its coming (Mark 1:8), Jesus receives it at his baptism (1:10), and it will be helpful in times of trial (13:11). Matthew adds fire to John's prediction (3:11) and concludes with a command to baptize in the name of the Holy Spirit but otherwise generally follows Mark. More often, however, these Gospels talk about unclean spirits. This helps us realize that their way of talking about the world is different from ours. They lived in a world filled with spirits. These spirits were always around to provide explanations for events, good and evil. Followers of Jesus got the Holy one. This way of thinking was just part of the general background noise of that world. Our challenge is to figure out how to translate it into our thought world.

Luke pays much more attention to the actions of the Spirit. This is especially noticeable in his second volume, the book of Acts. At almost any major occasion, the presence of the Spirit was crucial to demonstrating that the will of God is being followed. Luke is very practical in his approach to the Spirit. He regularly speaks about what the Spirit does but says nothing specific about who or what the Spirit is. Another interesting part of Luke's approach to the Spirit is that he never explains how he knows that the Spirit was present.

A few examples will be helpful here. In Acts 8:29, the Holy Spirit spoke to Philip. How did Philip know it was the Spirit of God? Luke never says. In Acts 16:6, 7, the Spirit did not allow Paul and Timothy to preach in Asia or go to Bithynia, but Luke never tells us how they knew this. On the other hand, in 10:44 the presence of the Spirit is made obvious because of the gift of tongues, so sometimes it is clearer than others.

On the other hand, we could understand this way of presenting the work of the Spirit as narrative honesty. Some people are sure about these things, even as they struggle to explain how they know. "Well, you can just tell," a student once told me. In this way, we can see that God's offer of the Spirit remains shrouded in mystery.

John's Gospel offers a similar sort of perspective. On the one hand, John contains many pronouncements from Jesus that are in plain simple language: "When the Spirit of truth comes, he will guide you into all the truth" (16:13). On the other hand, John's words always conceal as much as they reveal. The Spirit comes to guide us into truth, but how will we know?

So even the Gospels acknowledge diversity of experience. This means that what the church is offering cannot be put into single package. It is like a surprise package, where we ourselves are not sure what is in the box. There is Something outside ourselves, pie not just in the sky, but the ingredients of the pie vary. Some taste pumpkin, some taste quiche, and some taste kidney.

This offer, however, must be accompanied by a warning label. If we take seriously the ancient witness to the power of God working among us, we must also take into account the many references to evil spirits, unclean spirits, and the general active presence of evil. This does not mean that we need to adopt an ancient Jewish or Greek worldview in its entirety. This is simply not possible. It would require total immersion in both Hebrew and Greek as well as the return to a slave-based, preindustrial, agricultural society.

Once again we struggle with the issue of translating ancient wisdom into postmodern social structures. Yes, there is Something out there and inside us. It is a Mystery that can be partially comprehended, but at the very least we need to know that not everyone who claims to speak for this Mystery is really in contact with anything more than their own ego. This reality, too, is reflected in the Bible. Paul encouraged the church in Thessalonica to "test everything; hold fast to what is good" (1 Thessalonians 5:21). And the Elder advised, "Beloved, do not believe every spirit, but test the spirits" (1 John 4:1). So not everyone was as sure as Luke in their ability to judge whether the Spirit of God is present.

Once again, then, we find ourselves in a place of humility. While the church claims to be part of the family of God, we are always dealing in mysteries faintly glimpsed. And we can never limit the work of God to actions inside the church; neither can we claim that all actions of goodness can be attributed to God. Both of these are forms of imperialism.

B) ADDITIONAL THEMES

i) Jesuses

ONE OF THE STRENGTHS of the Bible that is so often missing in Christian proclamation is the variety of pictures of Jesus found in the New Testament. There are four Gospels, and each of them is different. This feature of the New Testament often surprises those new to it. Usually the church ignores this fact, and pretends the gospels are all "basically the same." This is true, depending on how broadly you want to define "basically," but emphasizing the commonalities also obscures the individual message each writer has so carefully crafted.

The effect of mushing the Gospels together is that each church picks and chooses between the Gospel stories to create its own Jesus, while proclaiming this as *the* true biblical story. This requires a certain amount of creativity, for one then needs to avoid or explain away the other parts of the Gospels that present a different picture, but since most people in the pews are predisposed to accept one particular Jesus, it seldom gets questioned.

This is, of course, not the whole of the situation. Besides these four Jesuses, the New Testament also contains Paul's picture of a crucified and risen Jesus, the very Jewish Jesus-in-heaven in Hebrews, the slain-yet-triumphant Lamb of the book of Revelation, and others. Each of these descriptions is different, and each is fully biblical. If we then want to add the various pictures of Jesus found in the early church and the later church, we quickly arrive at hundreds of options. It is like having a Jesus doll with hundreds of outfits from which to choose.

How does this work? Can we do that? Are we just free to pick and choose whatever bits we need/want to construct our own Jesus? Part of the answer to that question is yes. While churches often spend enormous time and energy attempting to enforce one particular picture of Jesus, the authority of the church in our postmodern world is limited. This authority has been breaking down from the moment literacy became a common skill and Bibles were made available in the language of the people. It has also been breaking down ever since political authority has been derived from something other than divine blessing. Since we no longer pretend that our government was specifically chosen by God, the government in turn has less reason to enforce the authority of one particular church authority.

So in that sense, yes, we are free to pick and choose. We do this anyway, so we might as well be honest about it. The Bible contains a variety of perspectives on Jesus, just as it contains a variety of answers to many questions. We can think of this as a serious problem or celebrate it as a gift, but neither perspective changes reality.

This was illustrated to me once in a discussion at church. We were discussing our church's response to the problems immigrants are having in our community and in America in general. In this discussion, people were assuming that the Bible was all about welcoming the stranger. So the

The New Testament—the good news

"correct" Christian response was thought to be hospitality, especially to those in need.

There are certainly many verses in the Bible that have this message, but the full picture is more complicated than that. There is also lots of xenophobia in the Bible. This is true in both Testaments. In the Old Testament, the book of Joshua is the obvious example, where genocide is the cure to the problem of ethnic differences. In addition, the books of Ezra and Nehemiah are very concerned with ethnic purity. But again, there are many passages about hospitality and welcoming the stranger. Lack of hospitality, after all, is the sin of Sodom and Gomorrah (see Genesis 19), and we know what God thought about that.

While most Christians would counter that the New Testament is all about love and kindness, the reality is not so simple. For example, in the Gospel of John, the disciples are commanded repeatedly to love "one another," but this love is not explicitly extended to those outside the community. This is why John is sometimes called the Gospel of Christian love and Jewish hatred. Matthew, of course, would have been distressed by this message, for he believed that those inside the church were Jews. Matthew is also clear that this love is to be extended even to one's enemies (5:44). But this love takes a very unusual form when Jesus addresses the Pharisees (see Matthew 23).

In contrast, Mark is generally more helpful, because there the insider/outsider distinction is continually broken down. The disciples (the insiders) are consistently portrayed as stupid and without faith, while a whole variety of outsiders comprehend and respond to the good news. So Mark is more useful to those of us who think the church should be continually trying to break down the us/them walls that divide us (national, racial, ethnic), but John is more useful to those who see the church as the pure community attempting to remain uncontaminated by "them."

When confronted with this multiplicity of Jesuses in the New Testament, many people respond with concern or even fear. Often this revolves around the question of whether anything is sure at all. Is the Christian faith really an "anything goes" proposition? Can you believe and do anything and still call yourself a Christian?

The answer to this is that there is a difference between variety and anything goes. Human beings also come in a variety of shapes, sizes and colors, but if it has four hooves and goes "moo," it probably isn't human. What the New Testament does is establish limits on Jesuses. Jesus was not a fully otherworldly spirit but was a real, physical human being. Jesus was not the one who brings esoteric wisdom that can only be understood by the elite but offered down-to-earth stories that can be understood by most people. Jesus was not a sword-wielding revolutionary attempting to establish God's kingdom through military action but instead died as a victim of the violence of others. Jesus was not one who hung out with the rich and powerful while condemning the poor for being lazy. There is a difference between multiple choice and making up any answer you want. In the New Testament, Jesus is a puzzle with multiple possible correct solutions but millions of possible wrong ones.

This knowledge should create a faith that welcomes multiple options. If we in the church wish to proclaim that Jesus it at least part of the answer to the problems of the world, the specific answer depends not only on the problem being addressed but the Jesus who offers a solution. For any particular problem there are various Jesuses who can provide help. There are also many options that are ruled out, things you shouldn't do. Not every question has "Jesus" as its answer, but it works surprisingly often if you're willing to be creative.

So sometimes you work within existing structures (here you use the stories of Jesus going to the synagogues), sometimes you work outside (here you use stories of Jesus doing his own thing with his disciples), but wiping out all existing social/political structures is not an option. Sometimes you respond with compassion (lots of stories here) and sometimes with anger ("woe to you, scribes and Pharisees, hypocrites," Matthew 23), but sitting in the background and whining is not the way forward. The choice of which Jesus to use in the story of salvation is the task of wisdom. We are still required to use our experience and our brains rather than simply parrot simplistic formulas.

ii) Paul—the first transformation

Jesus of Nazareth was a Jewish rabbi who wandered around Galilee, teaching in tiny villages. His message was directed toward the realities and problems of village life under Roman occupation. Soon, however, the message and the mission of Jesus got transformed and translated into very different circumstances. Even the Gospels are translations (from Jesus' Aramaic into the more common Greek language) and transformations (from Jesus' rural audience to the Gospels' urban audiences).

The New Testament—the good news

In reality, Paul was not the first one to transform Jesus' message. The early church in Jerusalem needed to make Jesus' message make sense to the people in the city of Jerusalem, especially the many who worked in the temple. The Jesus movement needed to deal directly with the temple and its functionaries and influence and must have translated Jesus' message appropriately. But Paul's transformation is the first one we have relatively direct access to, since Paul's writings are the earliest writings in the New Testament.

Paul also had the more difficult task of taking the Jesus movement and transforming it to be relevant to the culture of the cities of the northern Mediterranean. Paul was the one who translated from a salvation that addressed the needs of an agricultural village to a salvation that spoke to the realities of urban life in a significantly different culture from that of Jewish Galilee.

This transformation means that cultural awareness is as old as Christianity. Part of the history of the faith is the need to tell the old story in a new way, for a new purpose. Christian faith is always enculturated. This is true whether we tell the story orally or live the story in our lives. Both involve the possible acceptance, rejection, or transformation of cultural codes. There is always a sense that faith reinforces and/or challenges any culture's sense of normal.

The New Testament reflects both sides of this ongoing tension. The writer of Ephesians simply assumed that the Jesus movement was at odds with the political establishment around them (the "powers and authorities" of Ephesians 6:12), while Titus was to instruct his church to be subject to the authorities (Titus 3:1). Jesus himself harshly criticized all the rules and traditions of the Pharisees (Matthew 23:13–39) but only after commanding his disciples to obey these same traditions (Matthew 23:2, 3).

This means there is no such thing as "pure" Christianity. The various discussions and disagreements within the New Testament preclude this. Even the goal of purity is debated within its pages, with John voting yes and Mark voting no. This is great news. Purity is usually just an excuse for the accumulation of power in the hands of its enforcers. Too often it is also an excuse to persecute others who are less pure than "we" are.

On the contrary, any particular embodiment of the message of Jesus is always open to challenge from within the system. This could potentially create a church that is continually flexible in its message and its means. It certainly can be locked into particular forms through attempts to pretend its message somehow stands outside history, but these forms are inherently open to challenge from the New Testament.

So the Christian faith, insofar as it attempts to be a reflection of the New Testament, is always both at home in its culture and uncomfortable in it. American Christianity must be American but not so American as to be indistinguishable from the norms and aspirations of American culture. Various Christian groups will choose different aspects of local culture to promote or protest, but the tension created should result in movement toward a more whole, healthier culture.

The Easter bunny can provide an instructive example. In case you don't know, there are no rabbits mentioned in any of the gospels. There is also a consistent lack of chocolate in the stories of Jesus' resurrection. This does not mean, however, that either the Easter bunny or chocolate are evil or anti-Christian. It might mean, however, that corporations are attempting to turn an anti-empire story into one that celebrates consumerism and the commercialization of everything. The question, then, is not whether the church needs to engage culture, but how.

This is why we need to be constantly asking ourselves, Why are we telling this story in this way at this time? The nature of our promotion and protest should be clear and should be something that can be explained to any 10-year-old. This would create churches that know why they exist, and that are also open to challenge or cooperation. This should also create churches whose structures and activities are in line with its goals. This, too, is part of the ongoing process of transformation and translation found in the pages of the New Testament.

iii) Fearlessness

To begin to understand the nature of fearlessness in the New Testament, it is helpful to recreate part of the cultural situation of the early church. The word "church" itself simply refers to gatherings of people. In its earliest incarnation, the church was groups of people who got together to eat and drink. These gatherings had some connection to the life, teachings, or the death of Jesus of Nazareth. Nearly everything else was up for discussion.

The people in the cities and villages where these meetings occurred had a whole variety of responses to them. By far the most common response was ignorance. The vast majority of people in Corinth or Ephesus or Rome had no idea there was a Jesus-movement group meeting in the city, and if they did, they had no idea what the meeting was about. The church was just another tiny gathering of like-minded people in cities that didn't care.

Yet from this powerless minority group came the most incredibly bold statements. Quoting their Lord as saying, "No one comes to the Father except through me" (John 14:6), they proclaimed themselves the elect of the coming kingdom of God that would wipe away the Roman empire, establish peace and justice throughout the world, even to the point of transforming their physical bodies into perfect and imperishable ones (1 Corinthians 15:51–57). They also believed this message was a mystery, made known only to them (Ephesians 3:5).

Today, this message can sound incredibly arrogant, coming as it often does from a politically and socially powerful church. The message that initially was meant to encourage socially marginal groups to continue despite hardship and occasional persecution is now used by the politically powerful to maintain their positions of privilege. The words that initially emboldened slaves and outcasts now protects the powerful. What we are often hearing today is bottom-up statements coming from top-down institutions.

This means that these words no longer fit. They no longer mean what they used to. This is because language is always part of a context. Words are never uttered in a social vacuum. There is always someone speaking and someone listening, and these realities affect the meaning of the words. Words of freedom can become words of control, even when they are the same words. So these words in the Bible, originally meant as revolutionary, have now too often become anti-revolutionary. This does not mean, however, that the words no longer have anything to say to us. The encouragement to fearlessness is today equally important for the church. But now this fearlessness means something new. It means giving up power. It means giving up the security of social acceptability and privilege. It means the return of faith, which can only come when security is absent. It means leaving the religious fortresses we have built in the cities and the suburbs and looking for new forms to express the faithful church. This is the salvation of the church from what it has become.

At this point, it is also important to step back and note that this varies by church. Not nearly all churches today represent top-down power. There are politically influential megachurches and numerous official church institutions that look out at the world from the perspective of the powerful. There are also immigrant churches, gatherings of the marginalized, and even churches whose message and ministry is treated with suspicion and hostility by official society. And there are thousands of churches somewhere between these extremes, both reflecting and challenging the world around them.

For one group, then, fearlessness (and salvation) means giving up power, while for others, fearlessness means boldness. It is difficult to say which is more frightening. The gospel call to give up power ("whoever wishes to be great among you must be your servant, and whoever wishes to be first among you must be your slave," Matthew 20:26, 27) remains one of the most challenging aspects of joining the Jesus movement. This is both counterintuitive and countercultural in any culture. Why would someone give up power, privilege, and the security these bring? Why would someone exchange power for powerlessness? Why would you put down the sword and pick up the cross?

On the other hand, it is also easiest for the marginalized to stay quiet. After all, this is what they have been socialized to do. They have been told "their place" over and over again. There is a certain security in making these bold statements only to one another and not actually challenging the structures that keep them poor and powerless. After all, no matter how bad things are, they can always be worse, and challenging the power of the powerful seldom leads to ease and comfort.

The groups in the middle are also caught in systems that do not encourage fearlessness. Middle-class life is often centered on stability, which has both strengths and weaknesses. There is something healthy about living and raising children in a stable environment. But stability is always threatened by many forces. Debt, disease, unemployment, and a whole range of other factors constantly threaten the rather tenuous hold most people have on their current lifestyles.

People living under the threat of losing what they have are unlikely to act fearlessly. Middle class life teaches the virtues of caution, moderation, and staying safe. All these are the opponents of the fearless life. All these are also in significant tension with the gospel call to give up all you have and follow. So the church in the middle is stuck, and being stuck is the opposite of being free.

The New Testament's proclamation of fearlessness is a major challenge to all parts of society. It is also the only way to the freedom we so often claim and so seldom experience. Some of us are trapped in our stuff and our social positions, while others are trapped by poverty and learned helplessness. Both sides need the fearlessness that can come from trust in God

The New Testament—the good news

to be released from the traps they have either fallen into or constructed themselves.

Besides the general and widespread fearlessness needed to transform an entire society, the New Testament also proclaims another avenue into fearless living. This is the empowerment of those called to specific missions. I realize that using the word "mission" may have negative associations for many outside the church, but I'm not sure there is a better word for it. Hopefully an explanation will help.

The New Testament contains many unofficial titles for the various things people are doing. The twelve are alternately called "apostles" or "disciples." Paul prefers "apostle" to describe himself, but recognizes many other gifts within the church, such as prophets and evangelists and teachers (1 Corinthians 12:28–31). Later New Testament letters list other roles such as elders and deacons (see Titus 1:5 and 1 Timothy 3:10). Each of these roles is recognized, yet none of them is described in detail. What does an apostle do? What is the task of an elder? In most cases, it seems you get called, then figure it out as you go. In the early church, there are few set institutions but lots of workers.

There is also no sense that there is any limit placed on the number or type of roles. That is, there are elders and deacons, but that doesn't mean these are the only available tasks. An example from the earliest church is in Acts 6:1–6, where seven people were appointed to the task of food distribution coordinators. This role arose not out of adherence to a formal list of "offices within the church" but according to the needs present.

This form of organization can lead to various forms of fearlessness. If there is no one right way to do a task, and if there are no clear boundaries to the kinds of callings there may be, then both the individual and the larger institution has a lot of potential flexibility. This can lead to lots of opportunities to try new things.

This is true both individually and institutionally. Individually, a person called/appointed to an existing position can flex the position, since job descriptions are not rigid. Ideally, they should be able to do this fearlessly, since flex is built into the system. A system such as that in the New Testament is based on attention to both the gifts of the individual and the needs of the community. Attention needs to be paid to making sure there is correspondence between these, but otherwise the church should encourage fearlessness more than it discourages it (again thinking ideally).

Institutionally, the church should also be able to add and/or subtract roles, depending on either gifts or needs. I realize that institutions are by nature fearful things. Churches are no exception to this, and generally fear grows as time passes. One can often see the age of a particular church institution by the height of the walls between it and the world around it. But this fear is built into the nature of institutions, rather than being built into the nature of the church. After all, Jesus spent much more time battling religious institutions than he spent constructing them.

The example of Jesus also shows us that much (most?) of the work of God always has and always will happen outside formal organizational structures. God's activity is not limited by the fear or the lack of imagination within the church. This is especially important in a constantly changing world. The flexibility that arises from fearlessness means that task becomes more important than preexisting forms. After all, the nature of the good news proclaimed and lived by those called depends on the situation being addressed. So the task is not predetermined. Proclaim good news.

iv) Suspicion of human authority

Another theme in the New Testament that can be part of the church's contribution to the health of the world is the suspicion of the accumulation of too much power in human hands. Despite the many statements in the New Testament about power and truth and the coming kingdom, these are never linked to an increase in the authority of particular people within the church or the world. The New Testament's upside-down approach to power should always lead to bottom-up rather than top-down leadership, which then again deconstructs itself as those on the bottom begin to act as if they are on top. Jesus' example of washing the disciples' feet (John 13:1–16) shows us this upside-down power.

In the early church, suspicion or even hostility toward human authority made sense. For the church, it was never an option to be in charge. Most churches existed within the boundaries of the Roman Empire, and the empire was barely aware of their existence. More locally, the center of the Jewish tradition (i.e. Jesus' tradition) was Jerusalem, which was hardly excited about a rabbi from Galilee being proclaimed Messiah and Son of God. This meant that the church was largely a gathering of the powerless who had no more power together than they had individually.

The New Testament—the good news

This followed logically from the example of Jesus. Jesus appears to have avoided the cities in Galilee, spending his time in the small villages in the countryside. The Gospels say nothing about him preaching in the city of Tiberias, and they don't mention Sepphoris at all, even though it was the capital of the region. Even when Jesus went to Jerusalem, the home of Judaism and the center of Jewish power, he was clearly an outsider. When he went, it was as part of a crowd going to a festival rather than to teach or consult. And he was certainly more likely to encounter hostility than to be warmly welcomed by the chief priests and guardians of tradition.

Despite the hostility that Jesus was met with in Jerusalem, the book of Acts centers the early church in that city. This is a natural part of Luke's worldview. He seems to be one of those people who likes to have centralized authority. So for him, the church needed a single place from which power and truth radiated outward.

By the time Acts was written, Jerusalem was also a safe center, because it was gone. The Romans completely destroyed Jerusalem in 70 AD, and Luke is written after this event. So Luke could talk about that wonderful church in Jerusalem without needing to deal with the ongoing reality of that church's authority. The church in Jerusalem could function as a center in the book of Acts because it was also on its way to becoming myth. So the centralized authority of the early church was gone, and the book of Acts ends without the establishment of an alternative. Paul ends up in Rome (Acts 28:14–31), but there is no indication that he established an official headquarters. He welcomed people into his home (28:30, 31), but that is completely different from a governing council. So by the time Luke writes Acts, the church was without a natural center.

Besides a lack of centralized authority structure or location, the early church also had no central human authority that could not be challenged. The leaders of the church, James (Jesus' brother), Peter, and Paul all had different views on a number of issues. While Paul recognized the importance of the church in Jerusalem, he was also insistent that it had no final authority. Much of the book of Galatians appears to be a challenge to a version of the gospel that likely originated in Jerusalem (see Galatians 2:6). Ultimately, the Holy Spirit was in charge, and she blew where she wanted to.

Of course, all this is also simply historically necessary. The church was widely scattered, widely diverse, and most churches had limited email access. Jerusalem had been destroyed, so there was no point in pretending that it maintained authority. Some local and even regional authority developed, but the organizational structures necessary to maintain centralized authority were not there, nor would they be for hundreds of years.

The early church initially developed as a series of loosely connected (or even disconnected) groups that often had little in common. They recognized no specific geographic or human authority outside their connection with Jesus of Nazareth. Given better cell phone connections, they would have resembled the Occupy movement a lot more than they would the more organized churches today.

This attitude toward authority is also reflected in their response to the rulers and authorities around them. It is important to remember that the early church encountered a variety of responses from civil authorities. They were sometimes ignored, sometimes opposed, but seldom encouraged. Church leaders and members were well aware of stories of persecution even if they had not experienced it themselves. So Paul can speak of the need for submission to government (Romans 13:1) even as he spends time in jail. Obviously his version of submission is quite different from the mindless obedience to government too often proclaimed by the modern church.

Another key verse that shows the variety of the early church's responses to human authorities is Ephesians 6:12: "For our struggle is not against enemies of blood and flesh, but against the rulers, against the authorities, against the cosmic powers of this present darkness, against the spiritual forces of evil in the heavenly places." Here the assumption is that the church's interaction with rulers and authorities involves "struggle." Yet this verse can be contrasted with Titus 3:1, where Titus is counseled to teach his church to be subject to the rulers and authorities.

So the church began as an unorganized series of groups, many of whom were inherently suspicious of centralized power structures. This attitude also spills over into an inherent suspicion of nearly any human authority. It leads to a view of leadership that is unstable by design. The ultimate form of leadership is servanthood. Matthew 20:25–28 is the classic text but is far from the only one. In Matthew, Jesus contrasts the hierarchy of the world with the leadership from below that is to characterize his followers. True leaders act like slaves and servants. This potentially but logically creates a system where any attempt at exercising authority must be an exercise in nonauthority. Power is ideally demonstrated by one's willingness to give it away. This, too, is a form of salvation.

Paul appears caught in a similar predicament in 2 Corinthians in his dispute with a group he mocks as "super apostles" (2 Corinthians 11, 12).

The New Testament—the good news

He was never shy about claiming the authority of his call and apostleship, yet for a variety of reasons he did so in ways unlike traditional hierarchies. Paul proclaimed his authority based on his humbling himself (11:7), on his suffering (11:23–27), and on his weakness (11:30). None of this disguises the strength and authority that Paul demonstrated. But we miss the relationship between form and function when we forget the beaten, humiliated Paul. Modern leaders may want the mantle of Pauline proclamation of the truth but seldom are willing to "complete what is lacking in Christ's affliction" (Colossians 1:24) by taking on the whole of Paul's upside-down ministry.

In these ways, the New Testament both teaches and demonstrates a significant suspicion of human authority, especially in the accumulation of power by a few. Yes, there is privilege and status in being one of the saints, in being one of the holy ones, but these words are used to describe the whole church rather than the few special ones within the church. Ultimately, power and might are God's domain. The rest of us share the equality of servants. Yes, some servants have more status than others, but these are simply gifts given by the Spirit, which are to be exercised in a fashion befitting of servants.

v) The church itself

One of the questions that has been hovering in the background of this book is the question of whether the church is more part of the problem or part of the solution to the world's problems. My contention has been that there are resources inside the Bible to guide the church in being part of the solution and that, in fact, being part of the solution is central to the idea of being followers of Jesus.

So my answer to the above question is both ideally and potentially. This section is dedicated to flesh out this idea of the potential of the church. There is also potential for significant evil within the church, one it too often lives up to. I hope to convince you that the strengths of the church are greater than its weaknesses, which make it worthwhile to work with or within.

In thinking about the church, it is important to recognize that it is not one thing. It would be difficult to make significant connections between an American megachurch and the churches that meet in secret in various parts of the world. The number and type of contrasts between various churches could be expanded indefinitely. So what I say about the strengths of the church apply to some groups more than others. I hope to make my list sufficiently diverse so that some part of it applies to whichever church you are thinking of.

As institution

While problematic on a whole host of levels, the modern church can provide the institution and organization that could be very useful to anyone seeking to make the world a better place to live. Rather than needing to create the institutional structures that often accompany social movements, the church can provide pre-existing systems to organize, encourage, and empower large numbers of people. It is certainly true that modern communication systems are making institutions less important for organizing people and movements, but there is still something to be said for having dedicated, paid staff to provide full-time service to the tasks at hand.

Besides and possibly outside the larger structures of the institutionalized church, the local church has numerous strengths that are worth keeping in mind. Each church has a tradition of regular meeting, a spot on the calendar that people often keep free on a weekly basis. Because of this and other traditions, people often also have a commitment to the local church itself. The building also provides a stable place for gatherings, and these buildings are often empty much of the week. These are all useful pieces in any social movement, resources that are often untapped for purposes beyond institutional survival or the fulfillment of individual needs.

This may be truer in some places than others. In North America, the church, if combined with American entrepreneurial spirit, can create a foundational structure with potential to become what is needed for the times. In other places, institutional inertia may be too great to harness for problem solving. It is also likely that local congregations may be more willing to focus on local problems, whereas regional or international institutions may lack the capacity to shift focus.

Another reason the church itself is a natural ally in a movement to change the world is that churches usually already have some counter- or subcultural characteristics. Few churches actively encourage their members to live just like everyone around them. There is almost always some kind of cultural critique in the church. So the people in the church are preconditioned to think like this. The task, then, is to connect these tendencies to other or additional ideas.

As we noted earlier, churches exist in a wide variety of sizes, shapes, and types. This, too, is a positive aspect of church culture that can increase the effectiveness of any movement toward positive change. Variety is good. There are different ways at working at problems, with different local situations and different local solutions. Blue-collar churches have people who are used to going out and getting things done. Professional churches are used to working in committees and organizing various tasks. Large churches often have access to significant resources, while small churches have strong affinity and organize more easily. Each of these is potentially useful in creating change, especially when problems and solutions can be stated in ways that are congruent with the group's usual language.

This is not to overstate the role of the church in social transformation. Today's church is a mixed blessing. Its pre-existing structures can mean that a lot of work building an organization can be avoided. It can avoid unnecessary duplication of resources. On the other hand, institutions have a life and momentum of their own. It may be less work starting something new than trying to change or kick-start a church.

Then there is the larger question of whether institutions are really necessary for social change. Yes, they need to be brought along, or at least to stay out of the way. Occasionally they may need to be dismantled, and often they will have to be confronted, but there is a risk in overstating their value. Often the number of committees an institution has is inversely proportional to its usefulness.

One response to this is to recognize that saving the world will require many different approaches, tactics, and groups. There can be no single focus, leader, or group. It will require change on a vast scale, and quickly. So one effort is to help the church become part of the solution and then use its existing strengths to organize, gather, and act.

This will require churches to think in terms of task rather than message. They will need to define success in concrete terms that have nothing to do with the number of people who attend a worship service. They will need to think of themselves as training grounds rather than entertainment facilities.

I realize that most of the church will limp along, twenty or thirty years behind the times. Much of the church is still struggling to deal with the sexual revolution of the '60s, while also trying to deal with (or pointedly ignore) the new sexual revolution of the 21st century. This means that much of the work of saving the world will take place outside the church. That's great. Some people will be called to work inside the church, and many more will find their calling outside. Perhaps, however, these two groups can find common ground and work together whenever possible.

Ideally, the church can be *part of* the solution. It is not hopeless, but neither is it the Savior. It is neither Lex Luthor nor Superman. It is seldom bent on world domination, but it is also unlikely to arrive in the nick of time to save you from the bad guys. Much of the time it resembles the Pink Panther in action, bumbling along while often succeeding despite itself. Hopefully it is more comic than tragic. Partly that will depend on the willingness of a new generation of Christians to rethink the whole edifice, and reimagine the call to follow Jesus. There may also be some hope for those of us who are older. Neither group can offer its salvation to the other, but together we can become a significant force for the larger salvation we are called to live and proclaim.

6

Conclusion

As I walk down the streets of my town, I walk past many different buildings. Each one has its own purpose. Houses and apartments give people a place to live. Stores provide things to buy. Other businesses make things or distribute goods or services. Then there are the churches. There are lots of churches in my Bible Belt community. What are they for?

There are, of course, many answers to that question. That is not surprising. There is no particular reason why the various churches need to find a common goal or purpose. This has been true from the time of the earliest church. But whatever the stated or implicit purpose of a church, I hope they have two things in common.

The first commonality for the various churches is some connection to the life, death, resurrection, and teachings of Jesus of Nazareth. This is what distinguishes "the church" from other religious and civic institutions. This does not make the other institutions evil; it just means that they are not churches.

The second commonality for churches is that they should be a response to the real needs of its community. This is crucial. Churches should not *have* a response to their communities; they should *be* that response. When Jesus was asked which commandments were the most important, he named two: love of God and love of neighbor. Jesus also understood love as a way of acting rather than just a feeling in your heart. This love is enacted both individually and collectively. So our response as a church to the needs around us is one of the two things that make us a church.

These two commonalities also help us better understand the variety within the church. The New Testament has four Gospels (rather than just one). It gives us four different perspectives on who Jesus was, which gives us four options for what following Jesus will look like. When you add to this the picture of Jesus implicit in the rest of the New Testament, we see a church that begins in diversity and celebrates this in its foundational text. This allows the message of Jesus to address different people and be understood in different ways in different eras, but it also means that the variety of understandings of "following Jesus" only grows.

The communities in which a church exists also vary widely. This, too, began very early, as the small villages of Galilee in which Jesus taught were very different from the big cities where Paul started churches. So the church, as a response to its neighborhood, must reflect these differences.

All these are variations on the message of salvation. They do not arise out of a soteriology (understanding of salvation), neither do they lead to different soteriologies. They are the message; they are salvation. Salvation happens when we effectively and faithfully fix what is broken and heal what is wounded in ourselves, our neighbors, our communities, and our world.

In the interest of having this happen as much as possible, this book has suggested some resources for this task. My assumption has been that the larger task of salvation is already being addressed in various ways by many individuals and groups. The desire and challenge is not unique to the church. So the challenge of salvation is ideally a cooperative one, insofar as we can agree on goals and methods.

Still, there are some resources that the church brings to the task. It is not solely or uniquely qualified to bring salvation—in fact, it is also in need of salvation. Salvation is not something the church possesses. It is goal and task and process, dream and hope and desire. We are always part of "us who are being saved" (1 Corinthians 1:18). Yet in this situation, the church is not irrelevant. Insofar as we continue to work out our own salvation, this should prepare us to reach out to others, both those in need and those who have additional skills and resources (and often these are the same people).

If this salvation is going to function as salvation for ourselves and the wider world (including the mosquitoes), it is going to require two essential components: honesty and humility. I will leave it for others to judge how well the church has embodied these ideals. This will depend on what part of the church they have encountered. You can decide whether these are things the church needs to start doing, continue doing, or just do better. Or perhaps you already know churches that live out these ideals. In any case,

Conclusion

I offer them as ways for the church to move forward into a post-Christian, postmodern world while claiming (regaining?) its identity and call.

Honesty is the central component of any way forward. Throughout this book, I have tried to highlight two aspects of honesty that are crucial for the church. The first is honesty about the Bible-we-have rather than proclaiming the Bible-we-want. The Bible-we-want is a perfect book full of completely accurate historical (and scientific?) information that also contains the single correct answer to all our problems. Of course we want a book like this—who wouldn't? This is also easy to proclaim, since most Christians only encounter the Bible in predigested chunks at church or in carefully worded Bible studies that highlight the good and help us overlook the more troubling parts. It is also easy to proclaim because most people, when attempting to read the Bible on their own, find a world so different from their own that they have difficulty making any sense of it. So the options are to engage in an extensive, lengthy study of the socio/historical/rhetorical worlds of Jesus, Paul, and the various Old Testament writers, or to simply accept the version of the Bible presented to them in official church teachings.

This means that the task of honesty is not simple. It requires a cooperative spirit from laity demanding honesty, pastors willing to proclaim honestly (and possibly risk their jobs doing so), and professors willing to profess honestly (and also risking their jobs). There is considerable potential for pain and loss on all sides, as well as the weight of tradition and institutional inertia. So the reward must be real and important in order to overcome these drawbacks.

I am not suggesting that the Bible should be abandoned. In fact, the Bible-we-have is much more useful than the Bible-we-want. The Bible-we-have can lead to salvation; the Bible-we-want cannot. You cannot found a movement for salvation based on a misreading of your foundational text. Neither can you pretend that a book written by and for people 2,000 years ago can completely and in detail solve problems unimaginable in that world. It would be great to solve the problem of water pollution by having a prophet throw some salt in the ocean (2 Kings 2:21), but this is unlikely to work.

Still the Bible-we-have is useful. It provides resources and general guidelines in our search for a way forward, some of which I have outlined here. People around the world continue to find in the Bible the wisdom and strength to keep going despite the problems they face. They do find answers to difficulties in relationships, in the larger society, and in whatever life (or God?) throws at them. The Bible-we-have is a great book. It does not need to be set on a pedestal and hallowed. It has no value sitting in its obligatory place on a bookshelf. It is what it is, and that's all.

The second piece of honesty necessary for the church is honesty about God. The church needs to proclaim the God-we-have, rather than the God-we-want. God is not Santa for adults. God is not a heavenly vending machine waiting to rain goodies on nice people or those who ask in the correct way. Neither is God sitting in heaven, waiting for a specific sin threshold so that he can come and do the big entrance with the trumpets and heavenly armies.

The God-we-want arises from a natural desire to have Someone to fix our problems. This desire is easy to understand. It is also found within the Bible, as various parts project this picture of God into the past (like the Exodus story) or the future (Revelation). In each case, the author looks around, sees the mess the world is in, knows that this is far from ideal, and hopes for a God who fixes things for us. This is especially tempting at times when we feel helpless about our own ability to effect change.

The main problem with the God-we-want is that this God doesn't exist. So asking help from an imaginary God may not be particularly helpful. I realize that the God-we-have may help anyway, but this God is unlikely to respond in certain ways just to fit our fantasies.

There is certainly much about God that we do not understand. Speaking about God is always a matter of trying to find words for something beyond words. Even to call God "something" is wrong, but sometimes being wrong is as close as we are going to get. So no one can say for sure what God has or will do, or what God's "character" is. The issue at stake here is one of consistency. Those who have been waiting for God to appear in the sky to tell the world what to do have been consistently disappointed. Those who have been predicting the return of Jesus have been consistently wrong. Those who have been waiting for a repeat of the Exodus/Joshua story have been consistently frustrated.

Again, this is not to say that God has not showed up. It is simply to say that the God who showed up was not following the hopes and dreams of those waiting for the big rescue from the sky. The God who showed up did not rain fire and brimstone or appear with a flaming sword in hand. The God who showed up did not smite our enemies with plagues of gnats or send a golden city of Jerusalem down from heaven.

Conclusion

The church, if it is to proclaim the faithfulness of God, must proclaim the faithfulness of the God-we-have. The God-we-have shows up in times of need; the God-we-want does not. There is a definite place in the world for comforting fantasy, but the church is not that place.

Honesty about the Bible and about God should naturally lead to the second major component of the way forward for the church, humility. Humility for the church should be grounded in honesty. We need to be humble about who we are and what we know or don't know. We need to be humbled by the many horrible things that have been done in the name of the church and of God. We need to say "guilty" to the charge of hypocrisy.

Some people would prefer that the church simply disappear. Whether or not this would be a good thing, it isn't going to happen, at least not in the near future. In the meantime, a humble response is to get to work doing what we should have been doing all along. Or, for many churches, to continue quietly doing what they have already been doing. This may mean that the loony fringe of the church will continue to get most of the attention from pop culture and the press. Luckily the work of God is not dependent on popular acclaim or good PR.

Focusing on honesty and humility means leaving behind other answers, other responses to the world around us. Mostly these are centered on the idea of the big rescue from the sky. Whether this is proclaimed as God coming down to save us or us going up to escape the mess we have made (before or after death), they must be recognized as forms of escapism rather than as messages of real salvation. Only after we give up our exclusive claim to mediate salvation can we begin to actually participate in it.

Giving up the idea of the big rescue from the sky leaves us open to little rescues. It also opens us to the little (and big) challenges from a God who desires the long-term health of this world. This is not a question of God following us around doing the big or little things we want done. Hopefully it is a matter of us following God, the God-we-have, doing God's will (as best we understand it) with God's help.

These actions of following God's will are, then, cooperative venture between God and humans. So our task is to be open to that cooperation. This includes cooperation with other people, those inside and outside the church, contributing what we have and are to the larger task of salvation.

I realize that much of this is not news to many people in the church. For many Christians, this is cheerleading, giving them words and encouragement for a task they are already engaged in. But it will be news to some.

You Are Not Going to Heaven (and why it doesn't matter)

It will mean fundamentally changing their entire concepts of God, salvation, and a list of "religious" ideas they have always believed. This is hard work. It may take a long time. If this is you, I encourage you to be patient with yourself. The human mind was not created for rapid change, so God already knows the struggle and the time it will take. Hang in there, recognizing that this is your salvation, too.

HEAVEN

"I am not going to heaven." Let this thought roll around in your head for a while. Sit with it. Go for a run and ponder it. Let it be your final thought before going to sleep and see what kinds of dreams it brings. Say it aloud and find out how that feels.

I have been trying to suggest throughout this book that a good response to this statement is, "Whatever." My brother-in-law has for years been working out a theology and a life based on the phrase, "Oh well." Stuff happens. Some of it is good, some not. We try to do what is right, but sometimes we don't and sometimes even our good actions have unintended consequences that harm others. Oh well. This is true in life and may also be true afterward. Ultimately, what happens afterward is in God's hands. Jesus tells his disciples not to worry about tomorrow, for today has enough worry of its own (Matthew 6:34). How much more should this be true of eternity, which we can't even comprehend, never mind control.

In the meantime, there are things that need to be done. Life goes on. The worries of the day are usually sufficient for it. In response, we can sit and passively wait for the big rescue from the sky. Or we can lie and cheat and steal and kill, as ways of avoiding the real problems and probably creating new ones. This is true on an individual and a national and international level.

Or we can use the resources that God provides, in a spirit of honesty and humility, and do what we can to be part of the solution. This will usually also mean working together with others, for very few problems can be solved by ourselves. It will also mean cooperation with God, which should deepen and strengthen our relationship with the God-we-have. Abandoning heaven does not mean abandoning or being abandoned by God.

This book has been focused on a series of answers to a single question: Does the church have anything to offer the world? Too often it seems that the real answer to this question is no. The church is simply another institution that exists for its own sake, that exists to exist, to pay its bills and

Conclusion

salaries, without a discernible impact on its larger social world. It offers no real challenge to consumerism, nationalism, or the ongoing exploitation of the people and natural resources around us.

One response to this sad situation is to mourn and move on. This response is becoming increasingly popular in North America and Europe, as churches close or become museums and tourist attractions. Perhaps this is the best option, a necessary step toward honesty and humility.

Another option is to buy into the escape that the church is selling. So much of the energy expended in the church is focused on specific beliefs, things you need to assent to in order to be saved. The human mind is capable of believing all kinds of things, especially those that make us feel good. So we could just believe what we are told to believe and get on with life.

A further option is to focus on obeying the rules established by the church. This is often easy, since the church itself is more apt to talk about the sins of others. So as a married man, I may hear about the sins of premarital sex, homosexuality, and abortion and can firmly agree, knowing that these sins will never apply to me. The church in many places has retreated to the bedroom and is sitting there in the dark, fearful of being seduced by homosexual abortionists. This fear is so far from my lived experience that I can easily feel good about these rules, knowing they do not impinge on my life.

This picture bears no resemblance to the Gospels' pictures of Jesus of Nazareth. He was known as a friend to prostitutes and sinners. He traveled to people, rather than expecting them to come to where he was. He built no buildings, started no centers. He did not even have a house to call his own. He proclaimed a salvation that was a response to the needs of the people he met.

It is this salvation we are called to proclaim and live. It is grounded in hope and joy but also in reality, in the world-we-have, the Bible-we-have, and the God-we-have. These things are not incompatible. They exist alongside the scars of our past and the wounds of our present. A salvation grounded in a serious analysis of our current situation, realistic hope for and concerns about the future, and an honest look at the resources available is the only salvation worth pursuing. It can form the foundation for the message and mission of the church. It can also provide a foundation for a church that works alongside many other people and groups interested in similar outcomes. These other groups are often well ahead of the church in analysis, strategy, and tactics for creating change, for creating salvation. Hopefully the church can catch up.

www.ingramcontent.com/pod-product-compliance
Lightning Source LLC
Chambersburg PA
CBHW051949160426
43198CB00013B/2373